THE
POTTER'S
ODYSSEY

THE
POTTER'S
ODYSSEY

By Willard Spence

SUNSTONE
PRESS

SANTA FE
New Mexico

Printed in the United States of America
First Edition

10 9 8 7 6 5 4 3 2 1

Library of Congress Cataloging in Publication Data:

Spence, Willard, 1908-
    The potter's odyssey / by Willard Spence.
        p. cm.
    ISBN: 0-86534-003-X
    1. Pottery—Technique. I. Title.
NK4225.S72   1995
738.1—dc20   94-42857
                                                             CIP

Published by SUNSTONE PRESS
            Post Office Box 2321
            Santa Fe, NM 87504-2321 / USA
            (505) 988-4418 / *orders only* (800) 243-5644
            FAX (505) 988-1025

CONTENTS

PART V: GLAZES

PART VI: SANG-DE-BOEUF GLAZE

PART VII: SPECIAL GLAZE ADVENTURES

ADDENDA

ACKNOWLEDGEMENTS

In my own potter's odyssey I have learned much from many friends and students. Some are named in this book, and the others will know who they are.

My late wife, Louise, was a source of understanding strength through my long journey into clay and fire. She helped a great deal with the organization of the original manuscript and typed the first version. My daughters, Willa and Eloise, have encouraged and supported me in the decision to have it published.

I want to acknowledge the special connection I have had with Ghost Ranch and its Ceramics Program Director, Jim Kempes, for over twenty years. The Pot Hollow there has been like home for me. Ghost Ranch has provided a grant toward the production of this book through its Arts Team and Program Director, Dean Lewis, who has also helped arrange production details.

Finally, I record here my deep thanks to Melinda Lewis, whose editing skills made the book much more readable without sacrificing my intent or style.

Willard Spence
Taos, New Mexico
1994

ABOUT THE AUTHOR

In 1949 Willard Spence purchased an abandoned adobe, built by Pueblo Indians and called Na-Te-So, in the foothills near Denver, Colorado. He remodeled its decaying walls and opened his first ceramic studio.

At Na-Te-So he pioneered the development of special glazes, mixing over two hundred samples. Working with Clarence Jeglum, who was then a research chemist with the Philadelphia Quartz Company, he perfected medium-range zinc crystal glazes and developed a remarkable low-temperature iron crystal aventurine glaze. He also developed one of the first high-temperature aventurine glazes.

After training in theology in the 1930s, he spent some years in the Christian ministry. During this time he wrote *RELIGIOUS DIMENSIONS OF CONTEMPORARY PAINTING* under the direction of the late Paul Tillich, founded NICEA (National Institute for Contemporary Ecclesiastical Art), which held annual conferences at the Institute for Humanistic Studies in Aspen, Colorado, and edited the magazine *CHRISTIAN ART*.

Spence studied design at the University of Denver and the University of Chicago. Later, living in Taos, New Mexico, he operated the gallery Casa de Artes and was instrumental in the founding of the New Mexico Potters' Association. In addition to his work in ceramics, Spence writes poetry, which he has incorporated into his prose writings as well as published in the books *DESERT SEA AND SUBWAY* and *THE EAGLE FLIES AT DAWN*.

In the early 1970s, Spence founded the Ghost Ranch Ceramics Program near Abiquiu, New Mexico, where he still conducts workshops. He has also taught ceramics in Continuing Education programs at the Denver Center of the University of Colorado and the Taos Center of the University of New Mexico.

Spence has tested over one hundred local clays from Kansas, Nebraska, Colorado, New Mexico, and Arizona. He has constructed many kilns noted for their uniqueness and efficiency, including three designed at Ghost Ranch and four at a former studio in Arizona. He advises his apprentices to work firsthand with many materials and to "unravel their secrets for the added dimension of creative discovery."

In 1975 Spence showed three hundred hand-built stoneware pieces at Houston's Hotel Astroworld under the auspices of Ikebana International of Houston. This, he says, is the closest he ever got to functional pottery. Following the Ikebana exhibit, he developed his own porcelain as a vehicle for wheel work and special glazes.

Willard Spence's ceramic sculpture relates ultimate human meaning to our cultural malaise. His "Christ and the Missile" is displayed in Coventry Cathedral in England, and his "Broken Man," a life-sized fired clay sculpture mounted on a stainless steel cross, is installed as a permanent gift at Ghost Ranch near Abiquiu, New Mexico.

PREFACE

Odyssey—the word is paramount in this work. The book begins as an odyssey of the potter's emergence during the cultural threat of the last one hundred years. I use the word "rendezvous" to describe the conflict between potter and culture in their meeting.

Ceramic art is a three-dimensional entity robbed of its basic identity by two-dimensional media. It surrenders its basic essence by overcapitulating to painterly history. The potter survived the threat of extinction, however; working with clay in hand, the ceramist was too connected with earth to be submerged.

The very word "odyssey" suggests a wandering journey into the realities of shaping and firing clay with its attendant thrills. Actually, the trip is a thrust into the real world of discovery.

The intended purpose of this book is to facilitate discovery of the new by those who may need expertise. Even with so much ground covered by past exploration, the hinterland still beckons to the courageous person. But courage is not enough. There must be tools of mind and heart to empower the explorer.

This is not a how-to book. Many books about ceramics provide technique upon technique, tool upon tool, recipe upon recipe. Mastery of gadgets and quick, tricky how-to-do-it techniques may seem the way to go: everything is furnished and every question has a ready-made answer. But this leaves no place for adventure. This book has good recipes, of course, but it is really for those who will ultimately create their own new recipes.

The motivation is in the mind. Guideposts are necessary. They must be visualized. This book is written in the belief that the motivation will find the method.

"Journey To Earth" is not a trip to clay fields, but an understanding of what, in essence, clay is. "Journey Into Fire" is the story of clay reacting to heat. The chapter on the so-called copper red, Chinese oxblood (Sang-de-Boeuf), produced through deficiency of oxygen in the kiln, reconciles past riddles that have defied answers and delayed contemporary success. It proves the Chinese origin. More than that, it exposes the fallacies of the historical interpretation of how the kiln's atmosphere of oxygen is controlled. "The Iron Story" is the first work to review all of the facets of development in the use of iron oxide as a glaze colorant. The chapter thoroughly reviews all past, partial approaches to the many faceted uses of iron. It includes the celadons (reduced iron), the aventurines (iron crystals)—including one of the first successful high-temperature aventurines—and the whole family of Chinese Temmoku glazes, as well as special iron colors such as plum and orange.

The chapters on testing clay and testing glazes are as complete as any available. They have attempted to improve on the past statements of procedure, which are only partial. Chapters in "Special Glaze Adventures" include information on how to fire once instead of twice and how to medium fire ceramics.

Throughout this work my purpose and hope is to encourage and equip those who will continue the potter's odyssey.

Abiquiu, New Mexico.

PART I:

THE

POTTER'S

ODYSSEY

WITHIN

OUR

CENTURY

1

POTTER AND POT

In the final decades of the twentieth century, our culture is taking a long look at the potter and the pot, reassessing the pot as an art form. The potter is finding a new identity in the agora, the marketplace, which is not just for utilitarian pots but for all the things most treasured in our common life. Society is witnessing the resurrection of pottery from the oblivion of a past that has scorned and buried it as a hand-made art form. Perhaps now writing on the subject of pot and potter will find a friendly reception.

In the reassessment which follows, neither history, culture, nor philosophy can be ignored. Inquiry into the roles of potter and pot reveals the timeless reality of both in our cultural history.

The potter in ancient Chinese culture was usually anonymous. In some early cultures he was a slave rather than a free man. For example, in the social order, the Greek potter was a slave, probably more interested in his performance as a ceramic producer than in aesthetics or social acclaim. He was a day laborer, not a sculptor. But the potter of Cretan antiquity was accorded a place in the royal family retinue. The perennial interest was in the magic flowing from the potter's hands. The present day potter is a creator who, by the very act of creation, disdains the mass production methods of casting pots or stamping them out. Most technological methods produce no limited editions.

In short, the potter is a person working privately, producing by varied means clay shapes which are acclaimed both by people who love pots as art objects and by those who want to put them to functional use. The potter is basically an artist or poet of the earth.

The derivation of the term "artist" includes antecedents that suggest that it, like the term "craftsman," originally denoted skill. This linguistic line of reasoning implies that artistry is in proportion to skill, and that where there is skilled workmanship there is art.

The pot, in its essence, should be understood as an art object. Once formally identified and objectified as a representation of beauty, all the canons of aesthetics are applicable, not the least being form or shape. The pot's silhouette casts long shadows in the heart of the one who loves it. Its surface, decorated or not, impacts our visual response.

But being an art object need not negate the pot's functionalism. Our bifurcated responses make it difficult to evaluate that which is both an art form and a practical means to an end. Obviously, in early cultures the pot was valued as a vessel. How would water or grain have been stored without these containers? But both the potmaker and the decorator were esteemed. Many think of a mug for coffee or beer with salivary response, but gastronomic senses need not cloud the issue of aesthetics. Certainly the floral vase transcends its function as a receptacle for flowers.

The great ceramic decorations must be viewed as we see wall decorations, as projections of artistic reality, with the assumption that pot form and decoration have a harmonic unity. The need for a twentieth-century pot aesthetic requires an honest look at the facts of appreciation and at the critical standards that have persisted through the annals of art history.

For many reasons, the art historian's list of heroes places the painter rather than the potter in the limelight. An excellent indication of the subservient role of the ceramist comes from an assessment of the emergence of the Renaissance Man: there were princes, paupers, painters—but not potters. Gropius, of the Bauhaus School, remarked caustically, in a point well developed by Harry Davis: "Some branches of art were elevated above the rest, as a fine art, robbing all the arts of their basic identity in our common life."[1]

We do not insult Brahms or Beethoven by limiting the composer's accomplishment to his "skill." Nor should the Tang horse, Renaissance Majolica pot, or

Grecian urn carry exclusively a skill-centered connotation. The potter who probes deeply into the work knows the unique identity of that which remains a product of earth, air, fire, and water. The pot remains an art object, beautiful to behold, delightful to use, fashioned adroitly by hands of homo sapiens. As a product of earth's clay, moldable as wax, durable as stone, the human response to it is alive with meaning and mystery. The potter's art is a part of humanity's long search for the ultimate through aesthetic experience.

A long look at the history of art reveals that the glory of creativity in ceramics has never truly been lost. The renowned examples of cathedral art, the Gothic period, the neoclassical revivals, all seem at first to transcend the importance of the ceramist. Actually, ceramists have made an indelible impression on their cultures, for whenever archaeologists look beneath the burial grounds of culture, they find the folk potter, the ceramist, at work.

Let us not fall into the usual either/or traps, however. The pot remains as more than artifact. It is a metaphoric essence. We need no further debates on whether it be art or craft. As noted above, both denote skill and both are related to the beautiful.

Let us not be seduced into promoting diatribes against academic history nor into crusading for pottery's rightful place in the sun. No foray into the marketplace is necessary. Pottery's "problems," if they be that, result simply from failure to bring forth fruits worthy of the forceful impact of the medium. Intimacy, earthiness, plastic suggestibility are inherent in the mode.

The artist potter joins with other artists in expressing simple, abstract forms, a prophetic symbol for a complex, psychotic society. Clay and hand work may be seen as symbols of humanity's age-old need for a closer walk with earthly things. The emergence of the artist potter has its justification in the urge to create beautiful things with one's hands when the age is dominated by mass-produced methods. Thousands keep on going, barely eking out a living, seeking a way of life, a relief from the tragic frustrations of that awesome colossus, the machine age. Fads, styles, emphases in expression are all valid, but the pot remains in essence a statement of the human rendezvous with earth. Whether the potter's spirit be humble or not, the clay worker remains the poet of earth.

The populace is willing to be shown. There need be no professional jealousy in the citadels of art. The agora is free and open. If there is, in fact, a de-emphasis upon the role of pottery in the history of art, it is within the power of avant-garde images of contemporary ceramics to force a new mold into the modern consciousness. It is up to the potter to produce the metaphor, the image, whatever it may be, from the perennial realities of the clay with which the potter works. The pot must cast its vital image on a culture increasingly removed from the reality of earth. The ceramist need only build the imprint of clay itself upon the mind. The pot remains a symphony of function and form, of beauty and skill, an indestructible symbol for the culture that buries it.

2

THE ODYSSEY AS RENDEZVOUS

The word "odyssey" is appropriate for the journey of the American potter. Odyssey suggests a wandering journey and a wondering who we are and where we are as potters.

Gertrude Stein (1874-1946), dominant figure in art and poetry, believed life began with the twentieth century. She predicted ours would be a revolutionary, creative century; tables would be overturned. When she lay dying she cried out repeatedly, "What are the answers?" Later, she roused from coma to probe deeper, "What are the questions?"

Upheavals, change, new realities seem to have typified our century. Have any enduring realities emerged? As we near the close of the century, we do find identifiable truths emerging. The potter plays an important role in this emergence.

To truly understand who the potter is, we must not overlook some of the factors in the century-old journey. A short glossary may be helpful:

Mechanization: living in the machine age, with mechanical reproduction—a machine culture.

Milieu: environment and surroundings. It involves our cultural complexes, our societal emphasis.

Malaise: a part of our milieu, malaise is not necessarily a specific disease. It is bodily uneasiness and discomfort. There may be physical agony and lassitude.

Also note the word "boredom," which is a part of what it means to live in our mechanized, computerized society. There is a malaise from living in our cultural and technological civilization.

MILESTONES OF RENDEZVOUS

In the rendezvous of hand-made pottery production with cultural forces, the miracle is that the hand-made pottery survived. In the unfolding picture we shall observe the rendezvous in the following areas:

1. Our machine culture which, through its processes, dominated personal creative pottery and dictated canons of design.

2. The decorative tradition, in which the pot was often considered the means to an end rather than a valid object in and of itself. Ipso facto, pots were made as vehicles for decorators.

3. The folk tradition gave the potter in many lands deep roots from which to build. Americans often ignore tradition, belittle its values. Lacking strong roots in folk art, Americans often try to emulate countries like Japan and England, yet retain a unique individuality and freedom.

4. The general evolution of twentieth-century art history. Pottery tended to be dominated by the art tradition that used it.

RENDEZVOUS: EUROPEAN INFLUENCE

Morris turned the trek upward
For the craftsman
Got him back in circulation.

Yet the glacial machine age
The avalanche, the earthquake,
The volcano-spewed ashes
Like a blanket over the craft.

The artist potter stands deeply indebted to a man of wide vision and accomplishments, William Morris[2], for without Morris' genius the present movement might never have come. His genius changed the course of history in England at the close of the last century. He was a scholar and a poet, deeply interested in religion and art. His thinking on both art and industrial society was often at crosscurrent with much of contemporary England. While he was a Utopian socialist and dreamer, his practical attainments set his ideas to work in the social matrix. He set in motion his own factory where the worker was individual craftsman. He attempted to reincarnate the values of the guild system by installing the craftsman in his shops, in contrast to the England of his time. His restless genius resulted in original design in many areas of the house interior: furniture, rugs, tapestries, tile, and lithographs for books were all affected by his creations.

He met the needs of the home, and his business grew. More important, he gave status and recognition to the individual craftsman in an age in which such status seemed impossible. The craftsman assumed importance in the very era that had all but destroyed him.

It may be argued that to attempt to reinstate the craftsman is to try to turn back the clock. Certainly the colossal force of the machine age has run like a glacier over Morris' efforts. He did not succeed in changing the basic dynamic of an economic system. He did, however, serve as a historic symbol of survival in a machine age. Since his time, the hunger in the artistic potter for such individual expression has found new avenues of development.

Morris attempted to recapture the creative scope of the craftsman's birthright. He sought to return to the craftsman his inherent dignity. Yet the role of the craftsman diminished during the time of William Morris in spite of his efforts. His emphasis brought forward some very talented individuals. Some were scrambling for the painter's orbital position in the fine arts. Yet, with all the attempted revival, there was no essential alteration of emphasis by which individual craftsmanship of the potter could come to the fore.

There are those who feel that the artist potter is in a hopeless position due to the competition of industrial ceramics. The artist cannot compete with the machine; therefore, aesthetic value can best be served by using the artist as an individual industrial designer and by giving to machine-made products the best design that might accrue from the artist's contribution.

No less an authority than Dr. W.B. Honey of the Victoria and Albert Museum has echoed this point of view. Honey, as he compared the work of the studio potter to that of the industrial producer, saw a place in the industry for the art designer and even for certain forms of hand decoration. He pointed out that the craft-artist's method was not that of the industrial designer. The latter draws onto paper patterns that are mechanically produced, and never actually puts hand to clay. The industrial designer is concerned with methods of manufacture, producing ware marked by a clean and cold precision.[3]

One distinguished critic, Dr. Herbert Read, described commercial ware by three qualities: precision, economy, and simplicity. In his words, "The art of the craftsman is intuitive and humanistic (he performs nearly all of the processes with his own hands); that of the designer is for reduplication— rational, abstract, and tectonic—the work of the engineer rather than that of the artist!"[4]

And even Dr. W.B. Honey asks if there is any artistic advantage to clinging to handwork of the restricted kind in the circumstances of present day industry.[5]

RENDEZVOUS: THE DECORATIVE TRADITION

The epoch from William Morris to just before World War I marked a twin tragedy for the ceramic artist. Not only was utilitarian work overshadowed by factory ware, but artistically pots became simply tools for the use of the decorator, objects upon which to paint.

Many painters' decorations at the turn of the century were called L'Art Nouveau. Like the Jugendstil movement in Germany, this movement was inspired by a "return to nature." It was influenced by Japanese naturalism and the scrolled ornaments of the Renaissance. The Japanese designs had come into vogue after the 1867 Paris Exhibition, so understandably they had a decisive influence on the arts and crafts in France also.

The three-dimensional art of potters was overshadowed by this emphasis. Otto Eckmann was the chief representative of a floral style in Germany, with swans' necks, water lilies, vines, and aquatic movement. William Moorcroft, an English potter, used women trained in local art schools as decorators. De Morgan, a close friend of William Morris', was considered by many to be the first English studio potter. De Morgan's interest in decoration was at the expense of plastic form; he used Persian glaze colors for decoration as he labored for the grace of L'Art Nouveau.

The pre-Raphaelite movement, with Renaissance roots, applied lustre decorations, expressing nothing vital in clay form.[6] The decorative tradition was an imposed, patternistic development, deadening to all originality. The entire movement was devoid of creative clay design and sound clay construction. It was outmoded by the time of the First World War.

SALON D'AUTOME - 1907
Where was the pottery,
In the 1907 Salon d'Autome?

There was a potter named Mathey
His work was there
Was he at the grand opening
Or was he back stage?

His pots were decorated by Renoir,
Derain, Redon, Matisse, and Roualt.

Where's the guy who threw the pot?
He threw a chunk of clay out the door.
Back in the wings he
Had a potter's wheel.

With his wheel
He buried Nouveau.
Did someone throw a pot out the door?

RENDEZVOUS: THE VICTORIAN ERA

The arts and crafts movement of the Victorian era was eventually dominated by the "refined aesthetics" of the gentleman. There was discernment, hunger, and yearning for earth, potter, and clay. Perhaps the Victorian poet, Robert Browning, was more discerning of the hidden realities of earth, clay, and potter than we think. His expression of "passive clay" is provocative:

Ay, note that potter's wheel
That metaphor! and feel
Why time spins fast, why passive lies our clay,
Thou, to whom fools propound
When the wine makes its round,
Since life fleets, all is change;
The past gone, seize today!

Fool! All that is, at all,
Lasts ever, past recall;
Earth changes, but thy soul and God stand sure:
What entered into thee,
That was, is, and shall be:
Time's wheel runs back or stops:
Potter and clay endure.[7]

The popular beat for ceramics in the Victorian and post-Victorian period was in the boudoir, which has been defined as the ladies' private sitting room. Unfortunately, the expansive social role of women, showing such vitality late in the twentieth century, was not possible in the nineteenth century, so ceramics occupied a similarly cloistered position.

The leisure class in America had available an abundance of manufactured china on which to put low-temperature (overglaze) decoration. China decoration permeated the cultural life, first in cities such as St. Louis, later percolating into many hamlets. In one of these hamlets the author secured his first kiln in the late 1930s—a china painter's kiln. Carlton Ball, other potters, and myself operated some of these kilns as best we could to adapt to the potter's needs.

For better or worse, the field day of the decorator's art was to continue the emphasis on design from nature. L'Art Nouveau and Jugendstil were certainly the vogue, not only for the decorator but also for the factory. During this era, porcelains, china, and transparent ware such as Belleek were extremely popular. Many of us have inherited products of Wedgwood and other manufacturers from the china closets of that era.

Josiah Wedgwood played to the neoclassical tastes of upper class England, reviving the Graeco-Roman ideas percolating from the Florentine route in the Italian Renaissance. Like Moorcroft and De Morgan, he was called potter when he was really no more a potter than any other British industrialist of his time.

His use of division of labor, also an emphasis of the German Bauhaus movement, acted as the glacial sludge burying the craftsmanship of the individual person. Any true resurrection from the Wedgwood period must acknowledge the many unsung rural potters of the age whose tradition as folk artists had come down from the time of cathedral builders.

BOUDOIR
Wedgwood was the father of potters
Wealthy from playing
To social veneer,

With slip cast stamps of
Pretty faces of gods and goddesses.
Use a stamp for
Hermes, Demeter, Apollo,
Diana of Ephesus.

What pretty faces to
Tickle the matron's pulse.

RENDEZVOUS: BEACHHEADS FROM ELSEWHERE

Bauhaus from Germany

The Bauhaus movement, led by Gropius, began at Dresden and Weimar. With its roots in the philosophy of the German Werkbund founded in 1907, this movement faced the problem of the artist in industrial society directly and with courage. Its emphasis affected design and architecture, and Klee, Maholy, Nagy, Kandinsky, and other eminent artists were associated with it.

Bauhaus emphasized simplicity of form as well as functionalism. Certainly it affected American industrial design. But although the Werkbund did create a synthesis through cooperation between crafts and industry, in seeking full realization of mass production, division of labor, and engineering principles, it did not further the development of the individual craftsman.

The role of the potter in this was a part of the general emphasis. Noteworthy in the Bauhaus period is the work of Marguerite Wildenhain, a gifted potter who shaped ceramics in this design milieu.

Scandinavia

Many new developments in the twentieth century have brought the artist studio potter to prominence. The Swedish Society of Arts and Crafts began as a movement to improve industrial production and has encouraged a close collaboration of artists and industry for over one hundred years. The movement has not only inspired superior design but has swelled to become a social movement as a result of the lectures, exhibitions, study courses, and publications sponsored by the society.

The Swedish Society brought a number of younger artists into the industries. Wilhelm Kage and Edward Hald, pupils of Matisse, were among the most notable who entered the porcelain industry. Kage became the artistic leader of Gustavsberg Porcelain factory, where the slogan became, "More beautiful than everyday goods," and the public dubbed the style "Swedish Grace."

These ideas were fully developed by the time of the 1930 Stockholm Exhibition. Attention was focused on function and on cooperation with machines. The artist became more interested in stoneware than in porcelain. Stoneware heightened the artist's experience and cemented the bond between handcraft and functional ware, strengthening the consumer's confidence in the quality of everyday ware. Kage reflected this development.

Many of Sweden's best ceramists work as independent studio potters in their own workshops. Some have their own workshops within the industrial plant, using their best designs with industrial potential for the plant.

Functionalism brought the first major changes to Swedish design. Out of it grew many new forms made possible by use of stoneware. In spite of the revolutionary break with traditional style, Sweden has never lost sight of the value of ceramic tradition.

Finland has given the world many fresh and invigorating ceramic shapes, created as the handiwork of a number of outstanding ceramic artists. In nearly all cases, these works have been by artists who were in the employ of the leading factories. International exhibits have given a reputation to Finnish ceramics design that in the minds of many is second to none.

England

Bernard Leach, who appeared on the English scene about 1920, may be said to have fathered the English studio pottery movement. He was a skillful teacher in explaining exact use of tool and clay and the deft touch that brings charm to a pot. He was willing to give all he had to impart to others the grace of the oriental stoneware techniques.

Such people as Leach, W. Staite Murray, Michael Cardew, Pleydell Bouverie, and Norah Braden revived the potter's art in England. They have a message for the factory and the home. They speak of the right use of clay, of the reason for a pot, and its fitness for a given purpose. They feel the designer should actually put hand to clay and know the material.

Leach lived for many years in Japan and was widely influenced by Chinese, Japanese, and early English peasant pottery, although it was Cardew who rediscovered English peasant pottery. His emphasis was on the potter as an artist who can create pieces of individual beauty.[8] Cecilia Sempill writes, "The studio potters have brought us back to the personal charm of the individual potter's craft, and have shown their awareness of the traditions of English ceramics in relation to foreign influences."[9]

Bernard Leach many times preached the "Sung" tradition and commented upon the lack of a taproot in the potter:

"Adherence to Chinese standards are [sic] not what counts, but what we make of them. We are not the Chinese of a thousand years ago, and the underlying racial and other conditions cannot be repeated, but that is no reason why we cannot draw all the inspiration possible from the Sung potters."[10]

Leach is holding up a classical idea, that of history's best pottery. He asks us to be inspired, to absorb, to emulate in workmanship, not to copy. The craftsmanship evident in the Sung work makes of some of ours a bizarre cleverness.

This philosophy deserves a weighted consideration. With all of the tremendous influence of Leach, the interest he brought to stoneware and the Sung era, and in spite of many traditional viewpoints, England has its own restlessness. This restlessness, springing more from contemporary designs in other crafts, from perhaps a lack of color in stoneware, and from critics as well as artists and homemakers, has brought a new vogue into the English studio potters' work. Newer potters are thinking in a more contemporary way. Sam Haile, Lucie Rie, William Newland, and Nicholas Vergitte are among these. Influenced by African, primitive American, Minoan, and many other sources, they are using much more color and decorative vividness, together with a truly contemporary ceramic sculpture form.

Dora Billington, writing on these English potters, sees a wide eclecticism— Picasso, terra cotta, early Greek, and other influences. She welcomes the fact that "craftsmanship is not enough," although she feels British standards of workmanship have not generally been sacrificed.[11] Perhaps she is prophetic when she asks, "Why are we in this country so afraid of imaginative experiment?"[12]

RENDEZVOUS: AMERICAN INFLUENCE

The Slipcasting Era

At the turn of the century, there were talented potters at work in some American crossroads, some at Rookwood Pottery in Ohio. Though fine potters were at work there, the dominance of slipcasting seems to have placed the potter and his wheel in a kind of monkey cage for exhibits from the past. One potter from Rookwood built beautiful bottle kilns in central Colorado at a tourist crossroads. His genius brought world acclaim to floral pots with soft, mauve-toned, matted glazes. A potter was placed on display in a glass cage at the wheel, but no wheel-thrown pots were made or sold.

The tourist couldn't buy a thrown pot
The potter was back stage
The shaper had a sponge, a knife
And a clean mold.
The slip seam did not show.

Looking back, summarily, there were
A few potters behind the scenes
They were back stage for the show belonged
To industry, to reproductive methods, and to
Decorative tradition.

The tragedy, we repeat, is not the process. It is the willingness of the students to have the whole thing done. They create neither mold nor pot, design nor glaze. The only qualification is the ability to take up a pitcher and pour. Reminiscent of the china decorators in an earlier period, who found their joy in brushwork, perhaps the use of the brush was the only claim to personal expression the slipcasting participant could find.

The basic problem is the "stereotyping of originality." The method, though good, is rigor mortis to the hand. Certainly thousands from coast to coast have learned to pour. I have written a diatribe lamenting this reduction of the agility of the hand to a mere facsimile of artistic effort:

You want a mold?
Here it is, made commercially.

You want a slip?
Here it is, prepared for the class.

You want a glaze?
Here it is, ready made for you.

Slip, glaze, mold
Have no need of potter.

Discovering the Pueblo

A successful revival of Native American folk pottery has taken place among the Pueblo Indians since 1920. Some of the best of the current Southwest Indian pottery is made at the San Ildefonso Pueblo and the Santa Clara Pueblo north of Santa Fe, New Mexico.

Little is known of San Ildefonso pottery prior to a hundred years ago beyond what is revealed by the few pieces made in the last half of the eighteenth century that have found their way into museums and private hands. These pieces include some plain wares with black and red polish, the difference in color being due to the proportion of oxygen in the flame. These early pieces also include decorated ware—black on buff, black and red on buff (polychrome), and black on red. The black on buff was the more common form of nineteenth century pottery. Highly polished black pieces at San Ildefonso lapsed during the 1890s and 1900s, when there was a marked degeneration of all pottery due to the spread of American cooking utensils and the tendency to produce pottery for curio stores and tourists. By 1907 very few Pueblo potters retained knowledge of the old craft. In 1907 the School of American Research excavated the ruins of the Pajarito Plateau with the help of diggers from San Ildefonso, who made illuminating comments on the pottery.

In 1908 archaeologists uncovered some never-used prepared pottery clay and gave it to Maria and Julian Martinez, who made pieces from it. They also gave a reconstructed piece to Maria, asking her to duplicate it. This encouraged Maria and others to produce more high-quality wares.

Maria Martinez, Ramona Gonzales, and others turned out fine new vessels. Maria especially shone. She began with polychrome. As the potters progressed, the shapes and surfaces were improved, decorations were made more delicate, and the old-time polish was restored. Polished black pieces topped the market. In 1921 Maria's husband, Julian, whose famous decorations adorned her pottery, discovered how to leave a dull black finish to contrast with the black gloss: the famous black-on-black style.

The Native American method of firing reduces oxygen, using smoke from pulverized horse manure to create a dense black. The result can also be achieved with smoke from sawdust or old, damp straw. Recently another idea has emerged at San Ildefonso and Santa Clara pueblos: re-oxidizing areas, turning them back to a light color to highlight them.

Folk Pottery and Jugtown

The number of folk potters has declined as the artist potter increased in scope and influence. America, like England and the Scandinavian countries, once had flourishing folk potters. They were an integral part of rural culture, fashioning pots by hand for community needs. As the potteries increased in size and machine methods were introduced, the folk potters have all but disappeared.

American artist potters have been affected less by their folk potters than have their counterparts in England and Scandinavia. England's Michael Cardew has done much to carry on the peasant tradition in the style of his stoneware, while America's leading artist potters do not show much interest in the American folk traditions. Certainly we recognize the easy integration of the folk potter, who was as much a part of his community as the cobbler. We have already commented upon the impossibility of recreating the folk scene. Nevertheless, America has had to reckon with its buried folk tradition. For many, such a tradition brings a gasp of surprise. The folk potters of America, as those around the world, have continued their unfolding chapter, defiant of cultural atrophy from industrial nemeses.

In a secluded hamlet of North Carolina, near the town of Seagrove, Jacques and Juliana Busbee proclaimed a major role for Jugtown Pottery. Their dream, springing from a heritage of utility, gave form and color to handmade pottery. They pioneered statewide, and eventually nationwide, the rescue of this precious cultural heritage from decay.

The threat at the close of the nineteenth century was obvious. Everywhere china was available for the table. Glass jars abounded as containers for whiskey in a prohibition era. Carolina was headlong into industrialization. The Busbees were determined to revive the potter's art themselves.

They established a tea room in Greenwich Village for display of their ware. Young potters who could produce ware like that made in the eighteenth century were hired. Among them was Ben Owen, then in his late teens, who threw pots at Jugtown for forty years. He and others furthered the Busbee determination that pots must meet design and craft standards of excellence. Juliana Busbee attracted to the Greenwich Village store such celebrities as Eugene O'Neill and Sergei Rachmaninoff. Later, when the Busbees moved the business uptown, it attracted the patronage of Eleanor Roosevelt and the Rockefeller family.

Jugtown remained open through the 1960s, operated by Ben Owen and his brother, Vernon. In 1968 it became a non-profit organization, and the Owens still produce their ware as it was done in the Busbees' day. In 1980 potters were still at their craft in Jugtown. People who visit there feel the pots are more than relics from the past.

Perhaps a contemporary recreation of the folk scene could place the artist potter in closer association with fellow potters and the surrounding community. Bernard Leach has preached the value of the communal ideal to the individual's inner security. He mentions the great Chartres Cathedral as the result of artisans in truly human activity and lauds the social experiment at St. Ives, where a group of people work together in harmony and in the sharing of profit and experience.

FOLK POTTERS OF MAINE AND NORTH CAROLINA
The Busbees of Jugtown, North Carolina,
Lived where pots were made since the
Time of Ben Franklin.

With prohibition days
Who wants jugs?

With wood fuel and average glazes
They kept things going during
The great depression.

People started buying Jugtown.
New standards came along.
It was a people's art,
A folk art.

In 1934 in Maine
Fifteen families started working,
They were able to buy bread
With a hundred thousand pots a year.

They played at Blue Hill
With local ore and woodash for glaze,
The clay was on the hill.

Ever hear of folk art in America—
Busbees, Santa Clara,
San Ildefonso, Blue Hill, Maine?

Adelaide and Syracuse

Mrs. Adelaide Alsop Robineau, a china decorator, became dissatisfied with a process which did not include the shaping of the clay. Intensely industrious and open to experimentation, she procured her own kiln, pottery wheel, and other needed equipment and started working with porcelain in 1903 in her studio at Syracuse. She studied at Alfred University and later taught at Syracuse University. While operating her own studio, she founded the magazine CERAMIC STUDIO (1899), which later became known as DE-SIGN. Her incised ware became famous, and some of her porcelains were accepted by the world's leading museums. In 1910 she won the grand prize at the Turin exposition. That ceramic art does not hold a subordinate place to contemporary painting and architecture is certainly due in part to her efforts. After her death in 1929, her works were exhibited at the Metropolitan Museum of Art. It is doubtful if any American did as much to bring into being the American artist potter as did Adelaide Alsop Robineau. [13]

Much of the present day interest in ceramic art has resulted from the fact that people like Adelaide Robineau and C.F. Binns were vigorous educators. Binns, with his background in the Royal Worcester Porcelain, was a pioneer in the field of ceramic education. His own creations combined beauty and simplicity in utilitarian forms. [14]

Exhibitions, particularly by museums, have widened the influence of the artist potter. None have done more than the exhibits at the Syracuse Museum, founded as a memorial to Adelaide Robineau. These exhibits, no longer dominated by the works of a few exhibitors from a few areas, have increased the numbers of participating potters and also of areas represented. The periodic exhibit has included several commercial potteries and is open to the ceramic industry. In fact, the American Ceramic Society has held the annual meeting of its art section at the Syracuse Exhibit.

One critic at the Syracuse Exposition in 1947 was impressed by its upsurge and impact, feeling that techniques in form and design were distinguished and of ultimate historic importance. The main weakness he felt to be in the area of applied decoration and in the originating of basic forms. Decorations were often "trivial, eclectic, copied, remote, etc." Another writer saw "variety of characterization, totally different points of view, varied technique, and means used to secure variety. There is rich development in American ceramic art. It is unquestionably one of our major crafts. Our ceramic sculpture is second to none. Many exhibitors are leading industrial designers in America."[15]

3

TOWARD AN AMERICAN AESTHETIC

In the aforementioned agora (marketplace), we find a haunting presence. It is not Diogenes with his lantern, looking for an honest man. It is the American potter seeking an aesthetic. Has it been found? In this wilderness of contemporary life, with computers and jobless people everywhere, saddled by art from plastic containers, is the American agora a funeral pyre for pots?

The vigor of the American agora is actually a refusal to capitulate to funk art and pop art. Unaware of folk roots in the midst of mass-production machinery, the potter lives by a vital aesthetic. The poem which follows is a resurrection of the kind of question anthropologists do not dodge as they dig in the dung heaps of the past. What is the pot saying?

HOW COME
How come we are still around?
History has its ceramic dungheaps,
What will the super sleuth
Anthropologist say who digs a pot
Labeled 1982 or 1992?

How come there is still potter and clay?
Number twenty of millennia two,
Talking now of century twenty-one.
Most of the ten mad decades gone
And we're still around.
How come?

Hear the ring of the anvil.
There were few of us in 1910,
Now we are a chorus of many.

Travel the states of the Union—
Potters are working in old adobes
In abandoned farmhouses and barns,
Some nestle in brick kilns in Iowa.
How come we're still around?

The following conclusions may be likened to snapshots of pot and potter at this historic junction. Obviously we must be humble before what we see; what is said here may be further clarified by century's end.

1. The American potter came to the fore after the Second World War and is coming to maturity in the last score of years of the century.

2. The potter inherited a rich folk tradition, of which this American was, in general, not aware, denying the need of this tap root. The thing Bernard Leach and the Japanese artist Hamada used as cornerstones of their art—the essence of the peasant folk tradition—the American potter generally did not seek.

3. This ignorance of heritage does not mean the American potter was not deeply influenced by the force of native Indian pottery, revelling in its shadow in all sorts of free use of hand without the wheel, moving from pinched pots to burnishing. In no sense could the non-native potter rival the native work, but the joy of the work done on the surface and in the open fire was a new doorway of kinesthetic feeling. The Indian didn't feel threatened, as the intercultural communication was a shared value and a cultural bridge. The primitive impulse was basic.

4. Bernard Leach said much about the self-conscious individualism of the American potter. He felt our art to be riddled by egotism, suffering from exhibitionism. In this vein, Hamada of Japan mentioned the relief that he felt not only from folk identity but from what he called loss of self-consciousness. He called it "loss of tail."[16]

Clearly, we need to forsake some of the quick-trick, prize-seeking atmosphere of the show. The muscleman who wants worldwide recognition for a pot of colossal dimension may be misguided. However, the force of this person is a kind of driven energy our world needs and respects. Ego strength, when it is channeled to higher levels of refined expression, is a basic requirement of all achievement. The potter, with humble use of hand, can retain both head and tail without succumbing to bravura and its deadly effects.

5. In general, the work of the potter has resisted the demand for uniformity and conformity. The life of the pot has variegated and individualized. The impulse to exactitude was a crimping of the person, or a cramping of the style. It was a restraint on the imaginative force in the pot. Deviants from the norm, possible from exacting instrumentation of the kind used on the wheel in Japan, are not used.

The genius of pottery is indeed rootage. But the average American is not a taproot person and can never have the taproot used by Leach and Hamada as a supportive source. We are forced to admit that our expression defies unity. In fact, the variety of contemporary American expression is at present our reason for being. There are many who feel so intensely the genius of that lack of unity that they are impatient with anything else.

But lack of unity comes from lack of an inner vital direction—the lack of a vital center. The integrative force and power is lacking, and disunity is the result. The core is absent. The changing play of forces on the surface vitiates because there is no depth or anchor. A center is necessary. You cannot center the pot if you are not yourself centered. We would be most hypocritical not to admit the faults of wide experimentation, innovation, and imitation. We may play Indian and burnish. We plunge head-on into raku. We move from stoneware to porcelain, back and forth. America is everything. But being everything means that we are spread to a thin vacuity. To be everything is to risk being nothing.

Much said herein affirms the value of disunity in our art expression. There is much good in being able to represent "everything." Being everything has its advantages, yet we need the warning of the potential terrible loss.

Clearly, the direction toward unity must come from discipline of life and work. I do not advocate workaholism but a search into the core of soul for the meaningful response that leads to order instead of to chaos. Outer discipline is inner order. We create both from what we are in our solitude and what we are with others. The disciplined order of the apprentice system has been lacking. In the Orient there were apprentice relationships with their fruits. The fruit of discipline was great art. Discipline by itself is cold without this rootage in self and others. The rootage produces a beautiful flower. From it, growth begins. The root begets the flower.

The real flower of discipline is commitment: commitment to what one has discovered and what one wants to be leads to inner resolve. This resolve is a decision, a decision to follow. To follow is commitment. Commitment is the center.

"Americans come from many races and parts of the world. Who has a taproot? This cementing together of a thousand parts is America. A country like America cannot have one expression. It must have as many as the courses of its life. That is our genius. American potters cannot grow roots by imitating Sung or copying ways of life of the rural Japanese population. Conscious copying of the works of a culture unrelated to the mind and soul of our generation would produce a makeshift art. If we want the arts to be alive and even to grow roots, we must give freedom using every technique and type of material in the way one chooses. Man needs to find room for growth."[17]

Basically, America is a greenhouse system for new growth, new roots, new flowers. The American caught between the spaces of two oceans hears as in a seashell the echo of many cultures. The American potter does not surpass the Sung, but absorbs and builds upon it. The artist potter does not improve on the Sang-de-Boeuf reds, but gives them new applications. This potter does not disdain the raku and the tea ceremonial, but makes raku a venture revealing still more of the eerie configuration of raku glaze. The American recipe for raku is to do it. Try it. See it. Feel it.

The American pot claims no preeminence in humanity's long search for an aesthetic, except as it reflects America. The aesthetic is not for America. It is for the human race, for homo sapiens. The traveler to the moon gets a beautiful view of planet Earth, much of which is clay. The astronaut has touched dust that can never be molded as clay nor produce food to eat. The potter is, in a sense, a star traveler.

Once I felt in a pot that faraway twinkle in a star. The metaphor was not too different from the experience of potters led to an affinity with nature, "where mushrooms and sandpipers are part of cliff and sky."[18] I tried to picture on a pot a paleolithic drawing, framed by eroding wind and water to an ageless artifact. "The Chinese," said another potter, "have a word for what I try to express—'Mei Foon,' a simple and beautiful way of life, a harmony between the ethical and the aesthetic."[19] The idea of Mei Foon involves a totality of experience described as harmony. Within this harmony, beauty and ethos are juxtaposed. The simple and beautiful way of life is contingent upon a relationship with the ethical.

The American potter, in a world likened to the Banyan tree, appropriates a totality of world culture, yet in most cases falls short of that totality of harmony which accrues from the ethical segment. An ethical idea is invalid if it is not related to all of life. Its ramifications are for every person everywhere. Culture neglects no one. Ethics is not for one but for all. It springs from a life of social responsibility. Social irresponsibility is the result of personal irresponsibility—in therapeutic terms, tantamount to confusion. The opposite of this is responsibility, the cornerstone of therapy and also applicable to the artist and the potter.

The responsible potter looks deep into the heart of the person who responds. This person, from any walk of life, often unlettered and untutored, still has a basic inner response to the object. Couched in some such phrase as, "It's lovely, I like it, can use it for this or that," the response is ethical and also practical. John and Jane Q. Public do not buy what they dislike.

The potter is forced to come to terms with survival values as well as ethical ones. The communication between potter and buyer presupposes in both the quality of openness, which results in the ability to communicate or to build bridges. Truly the life of harmony, the Mei Foon, is the quality of bridging over. This gives the many roots of the Banyan a vital interflow of life.

OLD MAN TEAGUE
This year I'll be eighty-two
Fifty years here at this wheel,
Fifty years of glaze and kiln,
Turning clay from yonder hill.

Dug it, dried it, ground it down,
Churned it in the pugging mill.
Turned it, let it dry a spell.
Bisque-fired in a groundhog kiln.

Built this shop in twenty-nine.
Did what daddy said to do.
Jars and bowls and candlesticks—
Daddy learned me all he knew.

He got learned at nine years old,
Turning Rebel plates and cups.
Afterward, corn whiskey jugs
Sold real good. Those times were tough.

Daddy didn't last too long,
Only lived till seventy-two,
Least he got to learn me right,
Turn pots like the Teagues all do.

From Robbins clear past Why Not Church,
Here to Carthage, Steeds to Star,
These old hills have simply got
The finest clay. And there you are.

Finest clay and finest potters.
Coles and Cravens, Owens, Teagues.
Different families, different styles,
But Teague pots still look best to me.

Got my grandson at the wheel,
Turning pots. I showed him how.
He'll be good before he's fifty.
Must be thirty-seven now.

George Wallace
Mather AFB, California [20]

PART II:

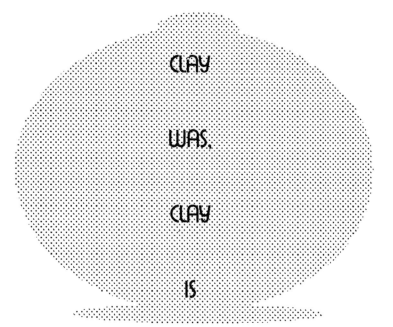

CLAY

WAS,

CLAY

IS

4

JOURNEY TO EARTH

I journeyed into clay fields
Letting the cry of the heart be primary.

My journey to clay was just such a sentimental journey. In primal conditions, against the backdrop of geologic time, my heart cried out, "Clay was!" Walking through those clay fields, I reached back from the living present to traverse something that was.

To be experienced as it is shaped
To be transformed as it is fired
To be tried in all sorts of experiments
To be used for man's benefit
To be understood in its essence and
To exclaim, "Clay is."

Calhan is a half-hour's drive west of what is now the American Air Force Academy, Colorado Springs, Colorado. I had heard stories of clay fields at Calhan, called "paint pots" by the people who live there. At the Calhan Paint Pots I ascend a giant syncline (geologic dome). The crust shows an area of many acres of clay. Formations break through in rocky ridges. Some erode into spectacular sculptural forms. Under this crust are vast areas of soft, eroded clay. One area is level and shows five or ten thousand square feet of pure white clay.

Walking through another exposure, everything is yellow, interspersed with green vegetation. I enter an escarpment through a tunnel of yellow. The whole arroyo is yellow, the yellowest clay imaginable. Further on I see violet, tan, red-brown. The colors are more than the rainbow's spectrum. The color bands build a symphony from the white backdrop. One hidden area is dominated by black clay—fireclay usable for firebricks.

My response is ecstatic. These clays were forged by weathering in time's cradle. I sense the aeons of time and space, the hand of nature—wind, water, freeze, and thaw—and the endless years it took for the feldspar to yield its impurities and become a silicate with alumina.

At Calhan is born an overwhelming clay urge, deeper than the desire for design or function. It is the desire to identify with earth, to see its essence, to try it out and discover what its mysterious combinations could yield as I shaped and fired. Before shaping clay we let it have its way with us. We become childlike in spirit.

I walk on through the undulations of the earth's surface, through acres where water from recent rains remains in puddles. I find clay in a pliable condition ready for modeling, finger it, start making abstract shapes. As it grows short, I add the local water. Returning in the afternoon I find the pieces leather-hard and safe to take home. But how to fire? With what to fire? And more than to shape and fire, deeper instincts ask, In what ways could this clay be used?

I returned and took samples from twenty-five deposits. I made samples into slabs and measured each for shrinkage, a true index of workability, measured in direct proportion to water added and to plasticity. I had read C.F. Binns' great book on the potter's craft.

The black clay, low in shrinkage and non-greasy, is fireclay, too coarse-grained for shaping. One test bar with a very high shrinkage came from a six-foot vein in the bottom of an arroyo. It was the only sedimentary clay found, greasy as lard. It was black from the carbons washed into it, and its plasticity was phenomenal.

After my class visited there, a student returning home to the urban sprawl wrote:

Earth I am,
It is most true.
Disdain me not,
For so are you.

Search for Clay at Ghost Ranch

Many artists have seen the clay fields near Abiquiu, New Mexico. Of particular interest are the deposits northwest of there at Ghost Ranch, an educational facility of the Presbyterian Church which has sponsored many ceramic workshops. It has been a mecca for study in geology, anthropology, and the arts, including ceramics. Ghost Ranch's nickname, "the magic place," is a tribute to the effect of this place upon seminar participants, who work together in surroundings of awe-inspiring beauty.

One sees here the red-toned badlands of sedimentary clay formed by an inland sea more than 200 million years ago. The 200-foot-thick layers would engulf all of the Calhan exposures. Capping the red-toned clay deposits is the purple-toned clay of the Morrison Formation. Above this are thick layers of limestone, and above this in many places is a calcareous gypsum material called the Todilto.

Earth scientists have written of these areas where the Morrison intercepts the Dakota Formation, which was formed above it at a later date. At the Ranch we were always intrigued by publications telling of a band of kaolin (white china clay) where the Morrison and Dakota meet. Would this yield workable clay?

I hiked with Jim Kempes, Abiquiu potter and fellow teacher of Ghost Ranch ceramics workshops, to the top of Mesa Montosa. It was a four-hour climb from the Ranch. We found in the Morrison earth great deposits of purple clay, but how to get it home? "We could get donkeys," Jim mused. Then we faced our own stupidity. It had never occurred to us we wouldn't be able to get the stuff down. "Well, let's not even take a sample home." Yet we reached the top of the Morrison Formation for a reason. Where the Morrison and Dakota intercept we found an eight-inch vein of white kaolin-like clay. We found kaolinite crystals.

We were reminded of the publications, which talked of kaolin deposits staked out and leased by a company intent on commercializing them. Two local men in the employ of the geologists took us to the exact spot. After a tedious and horrendous drive, we found the fenced enclosure and the ivory-white material. We took it home, soaked it, and pounded it, only to find it remained stone. It had none of the working qualities of a clay. In the laboratory of the chemist it analyzed exactly as kaolin. Did this make it kaolin? Put it in your porcelain, try it on the wheel, and give your own opinion.

In this hinterland of clay we had hit rock bottom with failures trying to find good, workable clay, easy to mix and use. Kaolin was nonworkable except where it was inaccessible.

Fireclay

We thought we might find fireclay, but always the vein was too thin, or too impure, or lacking in uniformity. When we found a thick vein, it was loaded with calcium-bearing yellow rocks. Did we get a good fireclay? Not as good as we could buy for much less work in Santa Fe. An engineer saw the black clay and said, "Let's process the oil in it!" He was referring to the black organic material which burned into a light color as the carbons were fired out.

Up the road ten miles from the Ranch, we showed some conferees this vein of black clay along the highway. (This group initiated the New Mexico Potters' Association the following day. The association still meets annually on Ghost Ranch.) One of the members from Los Alamos used this clay, firing about 2250°F. I admired her ability to use and fire the clay. It was workable clay, from a precariously non-uniform vein, and matured in the kiln 700 degrees below the fusion point of fireclay.

Earthenware Clay

What about the great deposits of red earthenware clay? These were red-firing, low-temperature clays. They formed a liquid glaze at stoneware or porcelain heat. But this clay lacked plasticity and could crack in drying. I used some of this mixed with fireclay for stoneware when I first moved to Taos. There was trouble. I found glaze particles popping off a month after pots were fired, a result of calcium globules in the clay which responded to atmospheric temperature and moisture by expanding and leaving ugly scarred pits in the pots.

As it turns out, capping these red badlands of clay were the purplish Morrison Formation and the tan sandstone strata, and overhanging them was the cap of gypsum. This cap dropped calcium particles from its overhanging pinnacles into the clay I was using for stoneware.

Glorious Values in the Search and the Mix

One of the hidden values of research is the glory of the search itself. Without the glory, research is an endless chore. With it, it is an adventure in learning nature's secrets. Let's list some values which came from the learning process of mixing clay with some other ingredient.

The Ghost Ranch earthenware clay mixed with fireclay worked at a higher temperature. Mixed with a super plastic clay, it ceased cracking. Mixed with the dreaded gypsum overhang, it gave us gorgeous, wine-colored decorative slip clay. Mixed with local mica, it has been used in low-temperature, outdoor, Indian-style firing.

We were experimenting directly with the earth for the joy of being a part of it. We were working with others in the joy and love of human company. Taking unworkable clay, learning its working and firing characteristics, making it workable—this was for potters the magic inherent in the Ghost Ranch "magic place."

One can, by searching, find a clay with especially valuable characteristics. We found this in a clay we called "Riverbend." It lent itself to sculpture. It would break up, "slack" when soaked in water, a necessary quality in local clay. But even Riverbend needed an additive to be at its best.

No doubt many potters and student potters may not find it practical to take time to mix local clay and may need to buy their supplies prepared. Even so, the "mix" is still important. The potter who would mix needs to know the whole process as he or she shapes and fires.

The glory of the atmosphere of earth, the glory of the search is hidden in the inner recesses of the ceramist's heart. Let's visit clay fields to escape from urban malaise. Let's journey to clay, the product of the earth. The search is its own reward.

5

EARTH HISTORY GIVES CLAY WORKING QUALITY

What in the physical makeup of clay gives it working quality? What is going on in the particles? The natural processes in the geological history of the earth that form clay account for its plasticity or working quality, and they account for the chemicals in clay that govern its melting point.

When clay is shaken up in an excess of water, the resulting suspension may remain cloudy for hours. The clay has formed a fine-grained gel. At one point, clay was thought to be more or less colloidal in its makeup. With the advent of the electron microscope, it has been found that many clay particles are less than one micron (one thousandth of a millimeter) in diameter. Further microscopic examination shows the particles to be flat or plate-shaped. A cubic millimeter of a very plastic clay might have five or ten million of these plate-like particles.

It is to be noted also that these fine particles carry an electric charge. If two platinum electrodes connected to over 200 volts are immersed in a colloidal suspension, a small current passes, and the colloid particles migrate toward one or another of the electrodes.

Apparently, three elements contribute to clay's plasticity: the plate-like shape of the particles, the particle size, and the electrical relationship between water and ultrafine particles of colloidal dimensions. Ultrafine particles in and of themselves do not create plasticity, as the particles will be touching only at their contact points or their edges. Clay particles, on the other hand, are a flat lattice, which allows much surface contact. During throwing on the wheel, for example, water acts as a lubricant, to enable the sheets to move over one another. They do not lose cohesion because of the electrical force of the hydrogen (H+) ions of the water. But an element of mystery still remains. The former president of the British Ceramic Society in a public address in 1957 stated that ceramists are still a little uncertain about what happens when they mix clay and water together.

Parent Rock

The outer crust of the earth, ten or more miles thick, has been radically disturbed by the pressures of magma, the hot liquid core of the earth. Mountains are the result of the gas-impelled expansion of this magma, some of which reaches the surface of the earth through volcanic action, faults, and other large-scale geologic movement. The material slowly disintegrates and is carried from the high points of the landscape to the low points by streams of water. The parent rock that forms clay is attacked from underneath by gaseous vapors of boron, fluorine, and other elements. The rocks most basic to forming clay (feldspar) are very susceptible to the action of water.

Two basic types of clay exist—residual and sedimentary. Residual clay is formed from disintegrated rock that remains in the area of the parent rock. Sedimentary clay is clay carried by the action of the water to other areas. Clay may be deposited in the floodplain of a river (fluviomarine), in a lake (lacustrine), in an estuary (estuarine), or in the sea (marine).

Water is the basis of most geologic change. It dissolves rocks, washes away mountains, leaches out soluble material, seeps into cracked rocks, and expands as it freezes, thus breaking the rock into smaller pieces. Weathered materials carried by water are subjected to an endless grinding action before they are finally laid down in river basins, deltas, or lake beds. The abrasive action that reduces particle size is absent in the case of coarse-grained residual clays. The sedimentary clays are reduced to grains of various size, dependent upon the action to which they are subjected. Marine clays form the largest clay deposits of any. They are the most impure of all the sedimentary clays. They are also the finest-grained, having been carried farthest by water action. They have accumulated from vast land areas and carry many organic remains.

Organisms and Carbons

The action of vegetation has an important bearing upon the plasticity of clay. Little or no organic material is to be found in residual kaolin or china clay. This is to be expected since it was never transported to areas where the earth was blanketed by vegetation.

The products of rock disintegration normally form soils in hot or damp climates. Clay may be formed, for example, in quiet areas where organic material becomes associated with it. This organic matter may become carbonaceous. In some cases, particularly in ball clays, the organic matter may be near an immature brown coal known as lignite (basically carbon and oxygen). Many of the fireclays were formed where the earth was destined to be covered by the great forests of the carboniferous period. They are sedimentary clays deposited in this period, before the action of the forests.

The carbonaceous matter in clay contributes to plasticity. The organic matter seems to act as a gum, helpful in plasticity, if not present in too great an amount.

Sedimentary clays, it may be concluded, are the result of transportation, in which they pick up and retain many impurities. This enhancement is induced by their small particle size, which is a function of the relentless mechanical abrasion to which water action has subjected them. The differences between these sedimentary clays and residual clays not affected by water transportation or vegetation obviously affect their plasticity.

6

EARTH HISTORY DETERMINES MELTING POINT

Let's return to the story of the earth's crust in order to observe the chemicals in the clay that are subjected to the action of nature. In this chapter we observe chemical elements, rather than physical factors (grain size, etc.) in relation to geological change. Geological history produces clays of a given chemical content. This content affects the melting point, or practical firing temperature, of pottery. Good pottery is fired to a temperature that does not exceed its melting point.

As noted elsewhere, the average composition of all the igneous rocks of the earth's crust to a depth of about ten miles is approximately 60% silica and 15% alumina. These essential elements of clay, which melt at high temperature, comprise about 75% of the earth's surface. The balance of the earth's surface is composed, on average, of iron oxides and trioxides (6.88%), calcium oxide (5.08%), sodium oxide (3.84%), magnesium oxide (3.49%), potassium oxide (3.13%), water (H_2O) (1.15%), and titanium dioxide (1.05%).

This group of minerals is present in varying degrees in clay bodies and can radically lower the melting point from that of a clay body containing mostly silica and alumina and more or less free from these impurities. One example of the latter is pure china clay. Another is North Carolina kaolin, which is 46.18% silicon dioxide and 39.5% alumina trioxide, with about 2% of the balance composed of the impurities from magnesium, sodium, and iron oxides. Without these impurities, an ideal or theoretically pure kaolin would deform at Cone 35 (1770°C or 3215°F).

A high-temperature fireclay from Amblicote, England with 45.22% silicon dioxide and 31.32% alumina trioxide, with impurities of almost 4%, may, because of grain size and other factors, resist deformation until Cone 35. Another clay from South Wales, 64.77% silicon dioxide and almost 10% less alumina, with a similar amount of impurities, deforms 15 cones lower than the Amblicote fireclay.

Residual or Sedimentary Clay

In terms of fusion temperature, clays may be classified into three types: high-temperature, medium-temperature, and low-temperature clays.

1. The residual non-plastic kaolins may be fired to Cone 30-35.

2. The sedimentary clays have increased benefits of plasticity from limited water transportation, but will withstand relatively high temperature because they contain limited amounts of fluxes and retain high amounts of alumina or silica. An example of this is the well-known Florida Lake clay (a plastic kaolin). The English ball clays were originally primarily kaolin from dissolved granite deposited in lake beds and estuaries in North and South Devon and Dorsett. The Devon is more pure than the Dorsett clay. The American ball clays from Tennessee and Kentucky, which are commercialized, become dense at 2400°F and begin to deform at 2900°-3100°F.

3. The low-temperature clays mature at temperatures under 2200°F. One example is a common red clay with about 20% impurities, often with over 5% in the form of iron oxides.

Chemistry from Feldspathic Heritage

A further clarification is needed of the effect of the parent rock on the physical characteristics and chemical content of the clay. Feldspar affects the chemical makeup of the clay. The clays formed by nature are the result of disintegration of granite and feldspar. Feldspar is a common mineral, accounting for about 60% of the crust of the earth. Feldspar contains alumina and silica, with one or more oxides of an alkaline nature (potash, soda, and calcium). Two or more of the alkalies are present, one of them in larger amounts. From this dominant alkali, we have one of the three general kinds of feldspar: potash feldspar (orthoclase), soda feldspar (albite), or calcium feldspar (anorthite).

The feldspars follow a general percentile because they were formed from a one-to-six ratio of molecules. That is, one molecule of alumina, one of an alkali, and six of silica. When feldspar is disintegrated by weathering, the soluble alkalies are carried off by water. The silica and alumina become chemically combined with water over a period of millions of years, resulting in a new chemical equation. From this molecular organization—an outgrowth of disintegrated feldspar—there is possible the kaolin phenomenon of coarse-grained residual clay, theoretically pure, amounting to the previously quoted 46.5% silica, 39.5% alumina, and 14% chemically-combined water.

In contrast, bentonite is a clay which has resulted from the disintegration of volcanic rock. Bentonite may not chemically differ much from other clays, but its physical nature is quite different. It contains very fine grains which assume colloidal character. It is used to lend plasticity to clay bodies. One percent of it in a glaze will give a flotation quality to the entire glaze. The result is a glaze that requires much less stirring when used.

Earth and Feldspar
Proportions of Alumina, Silica, and fluxes (approximate)

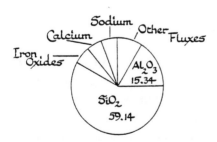

The Earth Crust

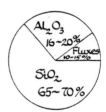

Feldspathic Material

7

WORKING CHARACTERISTICS
AND FIRING CHARACTERISTICS OF CLAY CONTRASTED

Building your own clay body is very difficult unless you are fortunate enough to have a clay usable just as it is. To build a pot requires knowledge of (a) working characteristics of clay, and (b) firing characteristics of clay. In short, how it works in your hands and how it fires in the kiln. The task is complicated by the fact that ingredients which make a clay workable are quite different from those which make it fireable.

What is relevant in assessing the working characteristics of clay is the degree of plasticity (working quality) needed to shape a piece by whatever method is used (throwing, coiling, slabbing, etc.). In addition, the piece has to dry satisfactorily without cracking or warping.

Essential to understanding the firing characteristics is the mix of fluxing agents (iron, potash, soda, calcium, magnesium, etc.) needed to initiate a lowered melting point on the alumina and silica (which melt above 3000°F) in order to mature and fuse the piece to desired physical strength and lowered absorption.

Working qualities (plasticity) are dependent upon the fineness and flatness of clay grains and the adhesive attraction between them in the presence of water. Firing characteristics are dependent upon the various chemical ingredients present, their amount, and the melting point of each.

Let us start with a finely-ground pint of dry clay powder. Place the powder in a plastic bag and work water into it until it arrives at a good working consistency. As you work the clay in your fingers, it asserts its magic. It does not change volume. It adheres together, assumes all sorts of new shapes. A mystery of molecular, electrical attraction holds it together. The magic of water makes it workable and moldable.

One test of plasticity is to roll a rope-shaped coil and bend the coil to a right angle. The coil should not crack at the elbow. Other adjectives describe plasticity, such as "greasy," "fat," or "long."

There are less subjective tests of plasticity. First of all, the degree of workability or plasticity is in direct proportion to the amount of water required to make the clay workable. Plasticity has been well defined as "water of plasticity." A plastic clay uses more water, so measuring water content indicates plasticity. An even better way to measure plasticity is through shrinkage: the degree of shrinkage is in proportion to the amount of water, which is in turn directly related to plasticity.

Returning to our point of finely-ground clay powder, we can throw the powder in the air or add water to it in order to form a watery suspension in a glass tube. The finer clay particles will float in the liquid (while the coarser particles settle) or will float in the air longest. Plasticity is in direct proportion to particle size, the finer particles resulting in greater plasticity.

The length of drying time is also in direct proportion to the plasticity of the clay. Dry a test bar, lay it flat—without turning it over—in the sun. Chances are it will warp as the side that is up shrinks ahead of the side that is down. The degree of warpage is in direct proportion to the degree of plasticity.

Take a test slab and hold it with your hands so that it can break near the middle. Bend it until it breaks into two pieces. A clay high in plasticity will have structural strength, resisting breakage, and will give a sharp popping sound when it breaks; a less plastic piece will break more easily and with less noise. Resistance to breakage, which we call "green strength," is in direct proportion to plasticity. The section on testing clay gives testing procedures in more detail.

We are now able to simplify and state a kind of syndromatic description of the physical or working qualities of clay. Plasticity (the quality that makes clay fat, greasy, or long) is in direct proportion to (1) water of plasticity, (2) drying shrinkage, (3) small particle size, (4) slow drying time, (5) warpage, and (6) green strength. Conversely, clays lacking in plasticity are "short" and "lean" and are noted for (1) less water of plasticity, (2) less shrinkage, (3) coarse particles, (4) ease of drying, (5) freedom from warpage, and (6) less green strength.

Satisfactory evaluation of clay can be made only by studio production conditions. Try a dozen or so pieces on the potter's wheel. Is the piece over-stiff or hard to maneuver from too much plasticity? Is it "buttery" from a clay with a greasy feel, responding very quickly to change, yet not holding its shape? This is a condition noticeable from a clay body with a substantial amount of kaolin. Is it "toothy"—that is, does the piece have coarse particles which help it to hold its shape without slumping? This is a condition noticeable from using fireclay. Is it simply non-plastic, too short to handle, breaking when subjected to pressure? This is a condition from using coarse-ground clays, lacking plasticity.

It might seem simple to consult the index of physical and chemical character-istics of clay and related materials to develop a perfect throwing body. One might add bentonite or ball clay for plasticity. One might add kaolin to give easier response to shaping. One might add fireclay to give tooth and structural strength. Addition of non-clay materials will make it buttery and also alter firing temperatures. But one cannot make these changes without other considerations.

Does the piece dry too slowly, and does it warp? If the piece is being hand-built, how does it respond to being rolled into slabs? Are the slabs maneuverable? A number of pieces should be tried to ascertain how the clay works in slab or in coils. Are there drying or warping problems?

Workability is dependent upon the grain size and plasticity—in short, physical factors. Fireability is primarily dependent upon the melting point of the chemicals in the mix. This mix is a combination of alumina, silica, and the so-called impurities that lower the melting point of the batch.

There are considerations affecting the melting point that transcend a purely chemical interpretation. It is increasingly recognized that a fine-grained clay will fuse more easily than will a coarse-grained clay. Coarser grained kaolins and fireclays, for example, tend to impede fusion because of the volume of the particle size.

8

ADVENTURE INTO MATERIAL

Often overlooked is the confrontation of the pot maker with objective material. Given a chunk of clay, a potter can both shape it and fire it. One writer suggested two types of potters: they were either mud daubers or firemen. That is, some love to shape and some love to fire. One of these loves is dominant.

The potter is aware that these materials have an objective reality of their own. Clay may resist or acquiesce to being shaped or fired. It may not work the way we want it to. Clay and glazes have their own way of responding to heat by exhibiting resplendent or unfavorable reactions. Hardly aware of it, the potter is baited to find out "what's going on" when clay or glaze does or does not work well.

The lure leads into deep water. The potter plunges in, searching eagerly for guideposts, experimenting, trying to obtain results. Coming up for a breath, the potter is on a long journey, becoming a discoverer, an adventurer.

Let us consider the implications of these concepts, followed by suggestions for finding the guideposts for which searchers and researchers long.

To be an adventurer or discoverer has more meaning to the potter than to be an experimentalist. The latter involves objective ceramic engineering standards, scientific procedures, and chemical equations. One may not have the will or the intellect to stumble about in what has been called "the wasteland of technical jargon." This can lead to a defeatism in which the oft-heard remark, "I am not a chemist," leads to a retreat to the shoreline, where others hand on a thousand well-known recipes or directives for procedure. This retreat is very unfortunate, for all of us have a deep love, if not for experimenting, at least for the adventure of finding out "what's going on."

It's a genuine thrill just to try some new mix of clay or glaze to see how it comes out. This deep curiosity reveals a love of the process. There is at work a "hinterland of adventure" which is more than experimentation. The potter is an observer who becomes the actor in the drama. To watch a glaze bubble and turn into its glassy phase in a raku furnace is to become the actor with tongs pulling the red-hot pot from the fire. The actor looks materials in the face and honestly asks, What are you in essence?, as the journey into clay and fire ensues. Helpless in his or her ability to describe the essence of a thing, the potter seeks answers by finding out how the thing works.

The adventurer's journey breeds great curiosity and motivation. There are dramatic examples of the journey as one forms and fires materials, as reflected in the experience of Pablo Picasso in 1960:

"At first nervous tension from the uncertainties of the fire—then he relinquishes his fastidiousness and rediscovers his solitude within himself—he experimented with the whole gamut of vitrifiable clays....Picasso's universe rebuilt itself.

"Because art is fluid and tangible, one should not get caught in standardizations. The wisest thing an artist can do is to express that which is his own....When I am quiet, ideas flash into my mind. The glory is in the search, not in the fulfillment."[21]

Guideposts from Materials

A mountain guide knows the trails that lead to a particular destination and is aware of crevasses along the way in which one can get lost. A qualified ceramic adventurer full of motivation and curiosity becomes aware of similar trails and crevasses.

As we shape, glaze, or fire, we are acquainting ourselves with ceramic materials. We may have a deep desire to learn of the processes, and even become involved in all sorts of experiments and methods. In order to discover something new, we may take a given material, mix it with another, shape it a certain way, or subject it to certain firing temperatures or procedures. We realize that:

1. The beginning point for all discovery is knowledge of a given material—what it is and how it works.

2. To arrive at this beginning point, we have to test materials in relationship to other materials.

The adventure is more than an act of will. It is an obsession as real as the alchemist's. We may plunge deep yet rise to the surface with nothing, unless we have knowledge of materials and how to use them. The kiln will serve as a relentless judge, revealing to us the laws at work that must be understood when materials react to fire.

In dealing with clay we must be single-minded. To know clay in its essence means to know how it behaves when shaped or fired. As far as clay is concerned, we must know both its working qualities (reaction to shaping) and its firing qualities (reaction to heat). The same is true of glazes. We shall be asking ourselves what a glaze is in essence and how it works. The potter, though not a chemist, needs a general appreciation of the factors at work in both natural and human-made materials.

The following summarizes the background on earth history:

1. Silica comprises about 60% of the earth's crust. It is seen as pure glass in quartz rock. It requires high temperatures to be melted.

2. Alumina comprises about 15% of the earth's crust. Like quartz, it resists melting at 3000°F.

3. Fluxes, often called impurities, are the materials that lower the melting point of silica and alumina. The most common are iron, calcium, sodium, potassium, and magnesium, which comprise most of the remaining 25% of the earth's chemical elements. Other fluxes are present in small amounts.

Natural earth has a molecular organization. This is why many materials, when analyzed, will show a constant percentage of given elements. An example is feldspar. As feldspar disintegrates, alumina and silica are combined with water to form clay. In pure china clay, most of the fluxes have been leached out. The presence of alumina accounts for kaolin's high melting point.

PART III:

JOURNEY

INTO

FIRE

9

SPAR

What is Feldspar?
Ask the engineer!
It's a 1-1-6 molecule.

How does the poet speak of it?
Spar is a musical word,
At work.

Mix in the spar
and start the heat.
Pot shrinks in fire
and breathes no more.
Heat closes pore
and liquifies.
The pot gets strong—
a ringing bell.

Spar is a family with cousins.
Potash and soda spar, cornish stone,
Nepheline syenite and volcanic ash.
What a family.

As a beginning potter, I went to see the work of students in the Colorado Springs Art Center. The instructor remarked, "We put a little feldspar in the Calhan clay. That hardens it. It starts the pot to fuse." What a beautiful, ringing tone sang out when the gorgeous bowls were tapped! The tone seemed to impart a musical magic to the word which kept recurring in my mind.

Feldspar! Feldspar! What is it? What does it do to clay? It makes it stronger! It starts a liquefaction process going around the silica grains in the clay. Volcanic ash, a spar cousin, does this at lower temperatures.

I drove through Norton, Kansas, looking for volcanic ash. I reminisced: this was the country where my father's father lived. He had mentioned the fine dust that blew from a mysterious substance.

At Norton I found a thirty-foot-deep, hundred-foot-long pile of a gray, very fine-ground material. The villagers said it was shipped out by rail and used for silver polish, and they told of a Kansas potter who used the gray dust pile for hardening pottery. Was this volcanic ash? Yes! I took my material home and mixed it with clay—two parts clay by weight with one part of the ash. I made it into small vessels.

Where to fire? I bought an old china painter's kiln. I filled it half full of pots and started the kerosene drip into the combustion pan. The kiln was for 1400°F work and I took it to almost 2000°F. Some of the brick dropped out of the floor, where the flames had built up the highest heat. The next day I unloaded the kiln. At least four of the vases had dropped 24 inches, landing on a concrete floor. Yet none of them had broken.

The Pueblo Indians use volcanic ash for what they call temper. At their low temperature it functions more as a filler than as a flux for clay.

I have walked through arroyos with beautiful white decomposing soda spar. I have seen the hard spar rocks on the roadside. I have traversed the feldspar beds at Custer, South Dakota, and watched the huge ball mills pulverize it. What Mt. Saint Helen's does now, the volcanoes of New Mexico once did. They were very active, and the finest grains blowing east were the slowest to drop. The very finest of the grains blew all the way to Lincoln County, Kansas.

At times I've used New Mexico ash from Bandelier, New Mexico. The New Mexico ash is similar to but not so fine-grained as the Kansas volcanic ash. The pile I got near Bandelier was soft enough not to require a hammer.

Volcanic ash makes excellent low-cost glazes. While potash spar works in clay at higher temperature, volcanic ash works somewhat below the middle range. The Kansas potter's trade name was "Melodies in Volcanic Ash." American potters are now using recently erupted volcanic ash from Mt. Saint Helen's. Many recipes are forthcoming.

What a family! It's the earth. Its work is done in the burn.

10

WHAT HAPPENS TO CLAY IN THE KILN

Potters trustingly place pots in the kiln without full awareness of their inner tension, naively placing the kiln goddess over the kiln, hoping that she is a benevolent protector, yet knowing the kiln is a relentless judge that overrules the goddess. They know that when the act is over, the judgments of the kiln are final.

Potters knows that they witness a drama, that their knowledge can only partially influence all that goes on when heat affects clay. Actually, the laws of chemistry behind the reaction of the varied minerals in a clay body, reacting as they do at different temperatures, are abstruse, complicated, and confusing. Nevertheless, we need to try to record a simple version of "what's going on."

Let us divide our drama into three acts: a prologue, changes of scenery during and between acts, and an epilogue.

Act I - Dehydration - Prologue

The first activity, which has to do with the loss of water, serves as a prologue due to the water lost and resultant shrinkage in the piece before it is consigned to the kiln. The plate-like grains of clay release first of all the water film between the plates. As this happens, the grains are drawn closer together and the water that had been absorbed into the mass of the grain—which acted as a sponge—begins to be released. The removal of water film and of absorbed water results in shrinkage.

A dense, fine-grained clay must be dried with great care. It must be dried gradually so that at no time will one part of the piece be drier than any other part. As long as all sections of the piece shrink together, no strains are created. A cup must be dried carefully, or the handle will dry and shrink faster than the cup proper and will crack away from it. Large pieces of clay tend to dry on the outside before the inside is dry. Then the outside will shrink faster than the inside and surface cracks will result.

In addition to water film and absorbed water, additional water fills the pores between the clay grains. Removal of this water does not cause shrinkage. Its presence cannot be determined by the color of the clay: the clay looks dry, but it isn't. At least fifty percent of the original water may still be present in a clay after it has finished its drying shrinkage. This mechanically combined water is removed by heating clay above the boiling point of water (212°F). Much of the water in the pore spaces and clinging to the pores is removed when the temperature is increased to about 250°F.

Potters usually leave a crack in the kiln door or have ample natural updraft ventilation to allow steam to escape as it is released from pots. "Explosions" can be avoided by firing slowly from 200°F to 350°F.

It is critical to allow sufficient time at these low temperatures: I suggest approximately two hours to reach 200°F and about six more hours to reach 350°F. This is a very slow cycle of only about 25 degrees per hour. Upon heating clay from 200 to 350°F, the mechanically combined and absorbed water is converted into steam and passes off. After the steam is released, the clay is dry. Even though dry, it could conceivably be returned to a plastic clay substance if removed from the kiln and wetted.

Clay is basically a hydrous aluminum silicate. As such, it contains water combined chemically with the clay mineral. Added heat in the kiln results in the loss of chemically combined water. The temperature at which this happens varies with the clay but may start as low as 650°F. Kaolin, for example, does not start to lose "chemical" water until about 750°F. It gives off water rapidly until about 975°F. Most of the water is lost by 1025°F.

Reference should here be made to the effect of heat not only on the weight of clay but on the volume of the mass itself. The loss-of-weight factor is most of all a function of the oxidation of the piece. The oxidation process, discussed below, starts at about the time the "chemical" water is lost. As organic matter distills without burning, the residual carbon combines with oxygen, forming carbon dioxide (CO_2), which is released.

Silica, the most important compound in ceramics, occurs in several mineral forms, one of which is quartz. At various temperatures, silica is normally stable; however, at 1062°F there is a sudden inversion of quartz from alpha to beta crystals. This transformation of quartz means a literal 1.03 linear increase, which is very sudden. A clay high in silica, particularly fine-grained, may crack if the temperature increase is fast.

During cooling the transformation from beta to alpha is also of critical importance. The glazes, which are rigid, may not be able to contract to the extent that the clay body does. Rapid cooling results in glaze compression "shivering," in which glaze pops off at the high points. This problem is partially controllable by slow cooling temperatures and by reduction of the amount of fine-grained silica in the clay.

Act II - Oxidation - Scenery Changes

Clays contain organic substances, materials containing carbon and hydrocarbons, in various forms. Wood and leaves burn out easily. Hard carbons, such as anthracite and graphite, require more heat to burn out. Anything that is combustible is burned, and all carbonates, sulphides, and sulphates have to decompose.

Changes in physical properties take place as oxidation proceeds. As the carbons burn, their color is bleached or lightened. A brown or a black clay may become light gray, tan, or white. The creamy buff or light-red color retained after oxidation is mostly a result of the iron oxide present in the clay.

As carbonates burn and disassociate, the piece becomes more porous. It may shrink some if the iron or other minerals that melt at a low temperature start to liquefy. This fusion process has possible significance if it starts before the piece has lost its carbonaceous content. The fusion that closes the pores of the clay traps the carbons into the mass of the piece.

During my early experience in working with fusible materials high in carbons, I thought a brick plant could be modernized so I made a sample brick. I used for plastic clay Pierre Shale, which was decomposed volcanic ash. There was a thin vein of this plastic clay running from central Nebraska to the Colorado Rocky Mountains. It was almost a bentonite. For filler I used a windblown loess. It was everywhere, and the nearest to brown dirt I could find. With these two materials used by the brick plant, I made the brick.

I showed it to a college class and dropped it on concrete to test its toughness. It broke in half. I had fired it in a day—the factory would have taken a week. It was black in the center, showing that the carbons had not burned out. All but the inner core of black had fired to a beautiful tan color. The surface may have started fusing before the carbons were burned out, a phenomenon that could have been avoided by a slow fire.

Generally, all carbons are released from a clay by 1650°F, although compounds difficult to break down may not dissociate until 1750°F. The fusion process may be underway, even though limited, at these temperatures.

Act III - Vitrification - Epilogue

The decisive action in the firing of clay may best be described as vitrification. In this process the chemicals present in the clay, often called fluxes, start to become liquid. At the beginning stage, the effect of this liquid on the unmelted material is very limited. It bonds unfused grains without appreciable decrease in volume of the piece or decrease in closing the pores of the piece.

This limited action results in a ceramic piece that may be called semivitreous— a state of incipient vitrification in which only the most fusible elements have softened. As the process of vitrification intensifies, the molten liquid formed attacks all of the unfused materials and takes the piece into a state of nearer complete solution. The liquid flows into the pores, making the pot denser, much stronger on cooling, and creating noticeable fired shrinkage.

As the kiln advances, the various materials (fluxes) that are fusible melt according to principles to be described later as "eutectic." For the present, it suffices to say that the kiln is forcing clay in an orderly progression toward liquefaction, which is completed when the pores are filled and the pot is dense enough to be rock-like.

Easily meltable components may be so liquid that the piece deforms before all pores are closed. Normally, a piece will be regarded as completely fused just before it becomes so soft it will no longer support its own weight. Tests will be shown that enable one to observe this point. Knowledge of the complete fusion point, or softening point, must be sufficient to prevent its occurring when valuable works of art may be at stake.

Vitrification Range

The aforesaid is an acknowledgment that the potter's art includes avoidance of "overfiring." The temperature range from that which fires pots to incipient vitrification (semivitreous) to that which results in overfiring (softening or slumping) may be defined as vitrification range.

Variations in kiln temperature should permit all the work to be incipiently vitreous but not overfired. For these reasons, vitrification range is very important. A kiln with known discrepancies in temperature is a real hazard.

A good stoneware body may have a vitrification range of more than 250°F. With this range, most kilns and kiln operators would perform satisfactorily. But factors producing vitrification may begin at temperatures much below the ordinary firing range. Clays fired to 2400°F may exhibit some initial fusion at a temperature 600 degrees lower, even though fusion may not be active until about 2200°F.

Clay and Vitriosity Curve

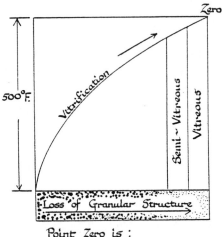

Point Zero is :
1. Total Vitrification
2. No Absorption
3. Maximal Shrinkage
4. Maximal Mechanical Strength
5. Clay Sags beyond zero point

Fusion may take place over a span of 500° F. or more .

Also, the reactions going on in a clay body need not be allowed to proceed to their completed state. Don't heat a piece until it is in its final state of vitrification. The solution of solids by liquids is fundamental. Dissolve only enough to fill the interstitial pores to a workable degree determined in advance. Conditions may require that one fire fairly fast. In this case, turn off the kiln when vitrification is proceeding rapidly, but lower the temperature before risking overfiring.

Because clays react slowly, time is a decisive factor. The time necessary to accomplish a given reaction in a pot depends somewhat upon the temperature. A pot held at a slightly lower temperature for a longer time may be as vitreous as one held for a shorter time at a higher temperature.

The Finished Pot

The final act of a kiln drama can place both the fireman and the fired pot under extreme pressure. There are other hazards from overfiring as the pot reaches its softening point. In the early stages of firing, porosity increases as water and carbonaceous and organic materials are given off. This porosity is lessened as liquids fill the pores. Air and gases can be trapped in the clay body as the surface vitrifies. There may be small disconnected pores which are very tiny but which can coalesce to form a bubble or blob (vesicle) that comes from incomplete oxidation or failures of decomposition. The incomplete oxidation can leave a remnant of carbonates or sulphates, which at high heat form gases that expand in the viscous clay. This is most noticeable in dense bodies. The gases may remain sealed in or they may force their way through the mass, leaving a series of connecting pores. Thus, at maximum vitrification, a form of bloating may take place.

There is a natural progression in the firing of a pot in which the hazards of vitrification are avoided. A clay body, free from difficult release of carbons, fired slowly, approaches and withstands the punishing temperature. It may move into its softening phase in a manner in which its true nature is revealed. With the softening phase, in which there is both liquefaction and decomposition, the true nature of an aluminum silicate shows itself by a progressive formulation of crystals devoid of the hazards of the over-fire. The kiln does not need to "kill."

The reactions between silica and alumina may be seen in progressive light as we approach 2200°F. The exact reaction may be only dimly understood, but we know that silica is liquefying, kaolinite is decomposing, and the activated molecular forces result in a new crystal alignment. In this crystallization a new identity is at work. The piece may change little in volume or weight, but it changes nonetheless.

The alumina and silica combine to form mullite ($3Al_2O_3 \, 2SiO_2$). At this point, all clays develop small, needle-like mullite crystals. They may be difficult to see with the microscope, and they may interlace. They give porcelain and other high-temperature bodies durable qualities. Mullite is stable and does not change until reaching its melting point at a higher temperature.

Mullite was first recognized as a distinct compound in 1924. Previously thought to be sillimanite, it was discovered in a laboratory but named after a natural material of the same composition found later on the island of Mull, Scotland. Mullite is an important compound in ceramics.

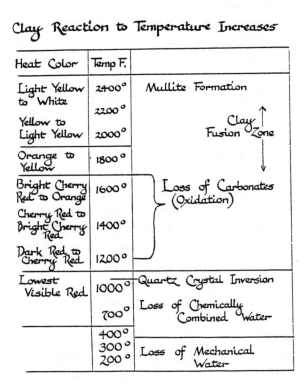

Clay Reaction to Temperature Increases

Heat Color	Temp F.	
Light Yellow to White	2400°	Mullite Formation
	2200°	
Yellow to Light Yellow	2000°	Clay ↑ Fusion Zone
Orange to Yellow	1800°	
Bright Cherry Red to Orange	1600°	Loss of Carbonates (Oxidation)
Cherry Red to Bright Cherry Red	1400°	
Dark Red to Cherry Red	1200°	
Lowest Visible Red	1000°	Quartz Crystal Inversion
	700°	Loss of Chemically Combined Water
	400°	
	300°	Loss of Mechanical Water
	200°	

Factors Progress Together at the Finish

When clay reacts with fire there are many forces at work. We need to reduce clay's behavior in the kiln to understandable patterns within a simple and progressive process. A test bar reveals an orderly process, a key to understanding the response of clay to heat.

Fired shrinkage is a key to what is going on. It is affected by the same factors that cause weight loss in a piece. Removal of chemical water and carbonization causes a slight expansion in the size of a piece. Quartz conversion affects volume slightly. However, fired shrinkage does not begin until vitrification starts. It is caused by surface tension of the liquids formed in the pores between the particles. In the small pores, the surface tension exerts very strong forces that pull the solid particles into a liquid phase, where they are totally surrounded by liquid and pores are destroyed. When this has occurred, further shrinkage is impossible.

The total fired shrinkage varies according to the type of clay. It may be as low as ten percent, while in some cases it may increase decisively without deformation.

Porosity increases rapidly in the earlier firing stage which releases water and carbons. In vitrification, as pores close the porosity decreases rapidly. The strength of a clay body is not much affected in the early stages of firing as water is lost. The alpha/beta inversion may even weaken a piece. Strength increases with vitrification and continues at a rapid rate until vitrification is complete. The secret of the strength is in the glassy bond that develops at the points of contact of the individual clay grains. In complete vitrification the liquid has formed a continuous bond throughout the body.

A well-vitrified clay will have a scratch hardness of about six on Moh's scale; this is harder than a knife blade. Scratching the clay with a knife blade reveals the degree of match hardness. As the temperature increases, the silica dissolved in the liquid increases and the hardness of the glassy phase increases. Obviously, as silica dissolves and mullite forms, both tensile and surface hardness increase.

Warpage is closely allied to shrinkage. Some warpage may be the result of strains set up when the piece was made or fired, or it may be the result of clay improperly mixed. It may result from the non-uniform application of heat. Generally, in a work made and fired without stresses, the essential warpage is a result of the vitrification of a piece to a softening point where it no longer can support its own weight. The warpage is due to gravity, and pieces must be made sound enough not to place undue strains on their supportive structure.

Several things are going on simultaneously in the finishing stages of firing ceramics: vitrification, fired shrinkage, loss of porosity (absorption), strength (density) liquefaction, and warpage risk from over-softening.

PART IV:

ADVENTURES

IN

SHAPING

CERAMICS

11

SLAB

I was invited by Ikebana International of Houston, Texas, to exhibit three hundred hand-built pots at a show in the Hotel Astroworld of Houston in 1975. I had only three months to make the pottery, which meant making four per day by slabs. The show opened up a world of meaning that transcended the merely functional in pottery.

Potters work for Ikebana in England, Japan, and elsewhere, creating works that become containers for floral arrangements in the Japanese tradition. To make a pot worthy as an instrument for ikebana, ikenobo, and the ensuing schools of expression, is to tell a flower it does not bloom unseen but is an instrument furthering the highest human sensitivities.

Humble as the pot may be, so long as it furthers its higher instrumentality as a container, it escapes into the rarefied air of originality. It somehow links up with the flower, the bud, and the stem, becoming a part of the mysterious totality. If the flower breathes the fragrance or echoes the linear heights of heaven and the horizontal waves of the sea, the pot claims an immortality of the earth. What else can the pot say but, "I am the mystical wedding of earth, air, fire, and water. By water I am workable clay, by fire I am tried to the temper of stone, through the air your senses perceive me as a kind of womb in which all the manifestations of luxurious natural splendor come into real being."

Many will say pots are only for mugs, bowls, casseroles, tumblers, pitchers, and all that is functional regarding the human appetite for food and drink. Long after these items have disappeared in the debris, there will be a few reclaimed by future excavators who recognize them as containers for nature's highest manifestations. These will transcend the aesthetic vacuity of late-twentieth-century American culture, like the Sung dynasty pots expressing the wedding of heaven and earth through the perceptual union of pot and life.

Since that first show in Houston, I have been besieged by mug seekers. I've made my share. Through the ikebana ideal, I gave free rein to other techniques. I want a pot to take fire like stoneware, hard as a porcelain, but I want it also to be a personal element in our impersonal world, and a prompter which, linked to other manifestations of nature, enables us to hear the heartbeat of the ocean sands and the pulsating wing of the diving hawk at dusk.

12

LARGE-SCALE CERAMIC SCULPTURE

Pottery has always included ceramic sculpture: the two are closely related. Some new areas of exploration in large-scale ceramic sculpture can be described using the following classifications:

a) Large coiled works, without an internal support (armature).

b) Works using collapsible armatures (polystyrene bead board).

Coiled Work Without Armature

A leading potter in this style is James Kempes, Director of the Ghost Ranch Ceramics Program, whose work is featured in some of the best of the Southwest galleries. These pots use coils $3/4$ to one inch in diameter, usually one or two feet long.

To apply a coil, first press it into place with the fingers. Since water is not used, maximal pressure is needed. Coils are not placed directly above one another; the Pueblo Indian style is to place pressure within and above the coil.

After completing five to ten coils, use the metal rib (Indians use a gourd shell). Supporting the inside with one hand, the rib is used with downward motion, then up and down motion, then cross motion. The process is repeated inside, and the rib, non-serrated, gives smoothness. Knives, trowels, and other tools may be employed. Longer coils expand the circumference of the piece; shorter ones will decrease circumference and control design. Design is also controlled by stroking with knives, sponges, etc. while supporting the opposite side with one hand.

With a marked decrease in diameter, the design approaches the diagonal. If it grows toward the horizontal the risk of collapse will be great. At this point, one waits a few hours for the clay to stiffen. Since this waiting process delays the total time, some of the exposed area has to be kept moist with a wet cloth. Sometimes a fine spray mist is needed.

Armatured Work with Polystyrene Bead Board

Ceramists have experimented with steel armatures and armatures of cardboard and other material. Unless one deals with zero shrinkage, the armature has to be removed or shrunk. Paper wads are of service to a point, but they have little or no supportive strength unless there is a framework within them. These materials, if not removed, have to be burned out in the fire.

The discovery of polystyrene bead board for armature is significant. The problem of clay shrinkage is solved by one of two methods in this instance:

1. Disintegrating the polystyrene bead board (PSBB) by the needle injection of a chemical that liquefies it to the point where the clay can shrink. What is not disintegrated by the chemical is burned out in the fire.

2. Removing the clay by cutting it into sections and removing the armatures when the clay is stiff enough to support its own weight.

Shaping the Armature

Polystyrene bead board may be purchased in large rectilinear chunks as much as ten feet long, available in lumber yards, building supply centers, and hobby stores.

The most common tool for shaping is a hard paddle painted with a quick-setting epoxy then sprinkled with carborundum grit. When the epoxy sets, the layer of grit is firmly imbedded. The paddle will really cut a swath on the PSBB. All sorts of tools are useable, particularly a wide variety of small and large saws. Even a hacksaw blade with a wrap of masking tape for a handle will do. Sandpaper is used for smoothing.

There is little resistance in the material, and it shapes quickly. We do not usually add to it, as we do to clay. However, it is possible to add. PSBB is glued and cinched with a small dowel stick pushed through. We usually only remove a little at a time so as not to take off too much. The clay is best applied by use of coils, but slabs and small rounded shapes may be added. The coil is not placed on the inside edge of the preceding coil, as in work without an armature; it must be on the outside. It is difficult for the coils to adhere when the piece extends outward. Sometimes this is solved by turning the armature upside down.

Use soft coils. For smoothing out the coil lines, use tools as directed in the previous section. Tools larger than the small rib work well.

When the work is completed and the clay is stiff enough, it may be cut in sections and removed. It may be advisable to cut the entire piece into two or more sections. After cutting the clay area, one saws through the armature with a large handsaw, using the line incised on the clay as a guide. An advantage of clay removal is that the armature can be saved for future use.

Armature Disintegration

Disintegrating the armature is often better than removing the clay. To disintegrate the armature, punch a hole in the clay with a large hypodermic needle or some similarly styled instrument. Make a nail hole for the needle. Injections of lacquer thinner are then made in rows one to two inches apart, with holes in neighboring bands staggered. The needle is put in just slightly farther than the thickness of the clay. One should experiment with the distance required between holes.

It is possible to inject just after cracking has started, but the best time to inject is after the clay has stiffened almost to the point of cracking. Generally speaking, it is best to disintegrate the entire surface. The illustrated designs will show points of tension problems. Disintegration of the core may be done in a few seconds by pouring enough chemical in the top.

Hazards

1. The lacquer thinner or acetone that disintegrates polystyrene bead board requires gloves. Avoid standing over it when pouring. If indoors, open windows. Better still, work outdoors to avoid fumes.

2. The flakes from scraping the PSBB are coarse and float in the air. Use a simple mask and work out of doors, preferably with the wind at your back.

3. When firing the material, avoid fumes from the kiln if they seem noticeable. A degree of ventilation should suffice.

4. Too much chemical poured into the clay enclosure will leave a liquid deposit on the bottom. This may soften the clay slightly. Placing open-bottomed pieces on a lattice work allows the polystyrene liquid to drain onto the ground.

13

THROWING ON THE WHEEL

In the past fifty years, the number of persons throwing on the wheel has grown from a handful to half a million or more. It seems there is a thrower on every corner. Likewise, the growth of efficient mechanical aids is phenomenal. In response to the needs of so many potters, commerce has produced machines for use in throwing, centering, firing, slabbing, extruding, glazing, and many other functions. These developments have been of much value to all of us, though they also call for critical evaluation.

Given the number of how-to books on throwing available, there is no need for detail here. But since the teaching methods for beginning throwers have been successful in the Ghost Ranch ceramics program, a summary of them is given here for beginners.

Avoid long hours at the wheel, but work daily for at least one hour. This gives maximal growth and minimal frustration. When you work, wedge at least three or four shapes so they will be handy when needed. Keep them covered to prevent drying. Have dry hands when you throw a piece on the wheel. When placing clay on the wheel, make a center ring by using a pencil or sharp tool about six inches in diameter. Hold the tool close to the wheel while it is in motion. This gives a guide so you will know where to throw the clay.

The term "throwing" is somewhat of a misnomer. When placing the clay in the center ring, you don't make a haymaker throw but a short throw from just eight to twelve inches above the wheel, while the wheel is not in motion. When using the method of throwing to create pots, emulate a lathe by the following modes of support:

1. Keep one hand always in some way touching the other hand.

2. Hold elbows close to body to give another frame of reference.

3. Use other frames of reference, including keeping hands securely encompassing the clay and, if possible, keeping the lower part of the hand in contact with the rotating wheel.

When applying pressure, emulate a rheostat. You are turning your tension or removing it by a very, very slow tightening or relaxing of muscle. The clay should not be at waist level but level with the end of the spine, or lower if the clay is between the legs. We avoid talk of centering clay but emphasize the fact that it is automatically centered if certain rules are followed.

Automatic centering is achieved by building two shapes, igloos and cylinders. Move from one to the other, up and down. This improves clay workability and teaches the beginning potter not to be afraid of the clay. After this shaping is done successfully a few times, the piece is, ipso facto, on center. The excess clay must be removed at the bottom by hand or tool. The portion of the hand best used is the corner of the palm closest to wrist and in line with the little finger. The palms, and never the fingers, enclose the clay. The fingers, extending beyond the clay, are joined, and the lathe support idea is maintained. One should make igloos and cylinders for several days before working with special shapes of clay.

Building the Central Cavity

Both hands should enclose the clay. If they do this intimately, the top cavity can start wherever the thumb touches, whether on the center or not. Also, with this position one can start with either thumb, both together, or one over the other. As the hole is worked down further, the hands come up higher on the piece. When they can no longer encase the piece intimately, another type of fingering is required.

When this motion is done, the resultant piece should be U-shaped, about an inch in thickness. The lower part of the sidewall should be no thicker than the top, the bottom no thicker than the side.

Making the Piece Taller and Thinner

After the shape is hollow, we are ready for an entirely different use of hands. We are ready to pull the piece upward and make it thinner. For this we use only the tip of the fingers—one or two fingers at the most—inside and out. Apply the squeeze at the bottom of the pot with a gradual (rheostat) pressure. The upward motion of the hand brings up the wall.

Water is not dumped or poured onto the clay but rather applied with a sponge. Also put water on that portion of the hands or the fingers that will be touching the clay. An equalized pressure will bring the piece up vertically. If the pressure on the inside dominates, the wall will move to form a belly or bowl.

Anyone can make a bowl, but it takes time to develop skill to move the wall inward. This requires dominance of pressure by the fingers on the outer wall of the clay. Not only is the pressure applied by the fingers in various ways but also extra moisture is put on the clay.

14

REDUCING SHRINKAGE

In the preceding methodologies of shaping ceramics, we have referred often to the problem of shrinkage. The basic problem is in drying clay without cracking it. Obviously, we reduce shrinkage by having less water in the clay and by additions of sand, mica, grog, etc. Also, we use less plastic, less shrinking clays. Lowered shrinkage often results in greater workability of the piece.

What additional roads are there to low shrinkage?

One major issue is the fact that clay for large-scale sculpture, usually on an armature, cannot shrink on the armature, so the clay cracks as it dries. Some special shapes need to be two inches thick or more, and a high-shrinkage clay is of no worth for this. I found that I could decrease shrinkage from three to six percent by increasing the grog. The best results were from using grog in two or three sizes, some lower than 20 mesh.

Jerry Rothman of California State College, Fullerton, has gone much further in reducing shrinkage, developing a clay that does not shrink. This is of incalculable value in permitting use of armatures. The zero-shrink works because of the way the water functions in the clay. Various chemicals are added so that the space the water occupies in the clay does not change as it dries. Most of his zero-shrink clay sculptures were made over steel armatures. The firing temperature was confined to the limit of the steel (2000°F).

CLAY
Are you there under the gray cover of stone
Must you be called by name to come?

Along the roadside giant scoops
Push you into huge vans

Contained in paper bags,
Do you groan when shipped far away?

Unfired! Unshaped!
Awaiting the hand of the potter
Whose forms fill the void of life
With fullness, joy and love.

The lone pilgrim
Takes your dust
Settles it with water.

You're drying
Shall I grieve, you're no longer a growing form?

Shall I grieve, knowing your freedom to grow is
Forever gone as you fire into stone
Unchangeable forever?

You're gone
But not the mark planted in my soul.

Your color—white, blue or gray,
Your name beautiful
Your feel so deep
That now you cover our world.

Outstretched arms receive you,
Gift of earth and potter
From earth's bosom—
Everything wears your gift.

Do people know you?
And do they see
Just who we potters are?

PART V:

GLAZES

15

WHAT IS A GLAZE?

The sands around the base of the explosion site of the first atomic bomb were melted to a glassy surface. Sand became a glaze as it melted. A glaze is merely a glass coating placed on a pot. The first glazes were accidental discoveries. Some may have come from bronze work, in which sand came into proximity with some flux containing soda, boron, or lead: some of the first glazes used these fluxes.

The first example of faience, using lead, can be dated to about 950 B.C., and a lead-silicate glaze has been traced to XI Egyptian dynasty (4000-3000 B.C.) Simple glazes have been made of flux alone on the surface of a pot. The flux then combines with the silica on the pot to form the glaze. Under the right conditions, a coating of lead on a pot gives a glaze, a technique used on medieval pots. Salt melted in a kiln releases its chlorine into the atmosphere and the sodium deposits fall on the pot (or the firebrick in the kiln) to produce a glaze. They steal silica from the clay body.

Chinese potters correctly inferred that some of the glaze on the interior of the kiln was the result of material in the wood ash that was deposited in the kiln. From this notion they constructed simple ash glazes.

A glaze may be seen basically as silica uniting with fluxes which lower the melting point. A well-balanced glaze, however, contains alumina which, with its high melting point, stabilizes the glaze and prevents it running off the piece. Some of the special glazes that require deficiency of alumina, Sang-de-Boeuf and the crystallines for example, are glazes that require very special handling, for they run off the bottom of the piece if there is depth of application.

Flint, or silica, is the essential glaze-forming agent in a glaze. Quartz, a crystallized form of pure glass, does not melt until it reaches over 3100°F, which is the melting point of silica. Were its melting point not so high, silica alone would suffice to form a glaze. Stoneware and porcelain bodies require a glaze maturing in the 2250 to 2400°F range. By contrast, earthenware clays require a low-temperature glaze, since the pot will seriously deform if fired at too high a temperature.

The term flux is given to those compounds which lower the melting point of the glaze. The most common materials used as fluxes in low-fired glazes are the lead oxides and the alkaline compounds—soda and boric acid (boron) glazes. They have functions roughly similar to fluxes, although they have varying degrees of effect on color.

The third ingredient required in a glaze, alumina, gives the qualities of durability and of resistance to abrasion and shock.

The glaze now has three basic ingredients: silica, the glass-former; a flux which lowers the melting point of the silica; and alumina, an element which gives increased toughness and hardness to the glaze and creates a higher maturing temperature.

The silica content is introduced into a glaze mostly through the feldspars, china clay, and silica. Alumina normally is introduced through kaolin and feldspar. The feldspars are minerals which contain alumina, silica, and varying amounts of potash, sodium, and calcium. The predominant flux gives its name to the spar compound, as in soda feldspar or potash feldspar. Feldspar does not work actively as a flux in the low-fire range. The fluxes unite with the silica contained in the clay body of the pot to form a bond uniting the body and the glaze. It is a tri-partite drama best understood by a pragmatic approach to the various functions. The accompanying diagrams show in a general way the dominance of flux functions in low-temperature glazes, and the dominance of the tougher silica proportion in high-temperature glazes.

Clay

Proportions of Silica, Alumina, and Fluxes
(approximate)

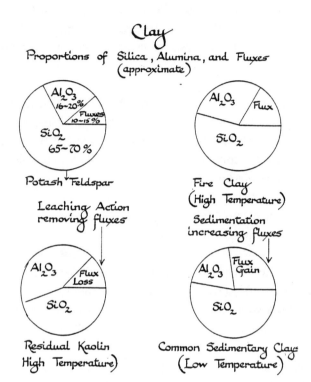

Al_2O_3
16-20%
Fluxes
10-15%
SiO_2
65-70%

Potash Feldspar

Al_2O_3 Flux
SiO_2

Fire Clay
(High Temperature)

Leaching Action
removing fluxes

Sedimentation
increasing fluxes

Al_2O_3 Flux Loss
SiO_2

Residual Kaolin
High Temperature)

Al_2O_3 Flux Gain
SiO_2

Common Sedimentary Clays
(Low Temperature)

Glazes

Proportions of Silica, Alumina,
and fluxes (approximate)

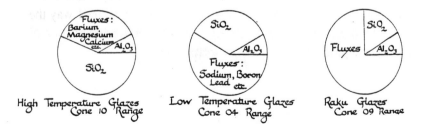

Fluxes:
Barium
Magnesium
Calcium etc.
Al_2O_3
SiO_2

High Temperature Glazes
Cone 10 Range

SiO_2
Al_2O_3
Fluxes:
Sodium, Boron
Lead etc.

Low Temperature Glazes
Cone 04 Range

SiO_2
Fluxes Al_2O_3

Raku Glazes
Cone 09 Range

16

KINDS OF GLAZES

Simple Glazes

Since we get remarkable glazes from very few components, let us mention some facts regarding a simple approach to glazes. There are the glazes that combine with the silica on the pot: (1) salt glazes, (2) glazes from painting on the surface with flux only, and (3) raku glazes such as colemanite with a small amount of nyepheline syenite.

There are many other simple glazes. A few examples are feldspar with wood ash and clay, colemanite glazes with kaolin and silica, volcanic-ash glazes with a small amount of whiting and clay, and potash-feldspar glazes that form at high temperature with a small amount of flux, such as earthenware clay or whiting. One gets some beautiful glazes from few components.

Complex Glazes

A glaze has been defined as a complex silicate. There have been as many as two dozen Sang-de-Boeuf recipes, each with from twelve to sixteen components. But such complexity is not required to give strong, rich reds. A Texas potter had a good Sang-de-Boeuf glaze using only soda spar, whiting, and colemanite in addition to the usual tin and copper. (See recipes in Addendum on Sang-de-Boeuf.) Neither the maxi-ingredient nor the minimal approach is ideal. I recommend glazes with six to nine components for the reds, because if variations exist in components purchased at different times they will be less noticeable than in a glaze with five or less components.

Lead

The most widely used low-temperature flux is white lead (lead carbonate). It is a powerful flux, giving brilliant color tones and glossy quality. It is not very workable above Cone 02 and does not reduce well. Red lead is not normally needed in a glaze. Lead stays in suspension in a liquid. While toxic, it is relatively harmless when handled with caution. It should never be used in glazes for tableware.

Alkaline and Boron

The soluble materials most frequently used in addition to lead are raw borax, calcined borax (only slightly soluble), and soda ash (sodium carbonate). Soda may also be used as sal soda, sodium bicarbonate (table soda), or sodium chloride (salt).

On dissolution soluble materials upset glaze balance, are difficult to store, and set up or stiffen in contact with water. Those who do not wish to live with the solubility problem may make or buy commercial frits. Nature's best frits are colemanite (Gerstley borate) and the feldspathic aluminum silicates. The brilliant alkaline turquoise glazes of antiquity were colored by copper in an oxidized form.

Frit

A frit is a glaze that has been fired in a crucible to form a glass and upon cooling has been ground by a ball mill into a powder. Soluble materials become insoluble in fritted form, and toxic materials are made safe. Fritting gets rid of things we don't need and stabilizes a glaze.

Frits require a special frit kiln. The raw ingredients are mixed together dry and placed in a crucible with an opening at the bottom (flames are directed against the sides of the crucible in other types of furnaces). Using a ball mill takes time. The only values I found in doing my own frits were in the improvements made in iron and zinc crystalline glazes.

A frit glaze is seldom a complete glaze for several reasons. Since a commercial frit is usually colorless, opacifiers or colorants have to be added later. The frit has little adherence quality, so a small amount of a plastic clay or bentonite is usually necessary. Adjustments for the final firing ranges also have to be made.

Salt

Salt glazing is done by throwing salt into the firebox of the kiln at the maximal temperature. The salt forms a gas mist that settles on surfaces of the ware. The chlorine is volatilized. The soda in the salt combines with the silica in the clay to form a tough glaze. Salt glazes on stoneware are excellent at temperatures from Cone 4 to Cone 9. On flat surfaces salt glazing produces a less undulant and smoother texture.

The salt glaze procedure is simple. At body-maturing temperature, common salt is thrown into the firebox or through ports entering the kiln chamber. Unfortunately, salt glazes the brick in the kiln as well.

Slip Glazes

Slip glazes are made by using a low-firing clay as glaze on a higher-firing clay. Albany slip and Barnard slip work well for this, as slips do well at high temperatures. All slip glazes are made from raw natural clays which contain sufficient fluxes to function as glazes without much further preparation.

Lustre

Lustre glazes have a beautiful iridescence that lights the surface. This lustre is obtained by depositing a thin film of metal on top of the glaze so that it refracts light in a manner reminiscent of the colors generated by oil on water.

Lustres require reduction, an oxygen-deficient firing atmosphere. Sometimes this is accomplished by manipulating the fire and sometimes by introducing organic matter such as mothballs into the glaze. Successful lustre glazes involve particular types of glazes under the lustre. To make successful lustres is a most complicated process. The reader is referred to Dr. Herbert H. Saunder's work for a detailed discussion.[22]

Ash Glazes

Ash glazes give beautiful textures and finish. They are economical, and preparation is fairly simple. In order to prepare an ash glaze, one assumes the presence of such materials as all the usual fluxes, with alumina, and a fairly high silica content.

Since the potter is working with an unknown fusion point and chemical content, a trial batch of equal parts of ash, kaolin, and feldspar, as suggested by Bernard Leach, is recommended. If the piece looks like alligator skin or has a matte effect, reduce kaolin and increase feldspar. Triaxial diagrams with several mixes and combinations may be useful, or just try one or two altered recipes. In my experience, one or two alterations are sufficient to secure a good glossy glaze. Following this, other fluxes may be added—dolomite, zinc, colemanite, etc.

Crackle Glazes

Crackle glazes are the result of differences in the coefficient of expansion of clay body and glaze. In crazing, the glaze is tensed by being stretched under conditions of temperature change that cause contraction and expansion of clay and glaze. A crackle is one which leaves oversized cracks when crazing.

Crackles may be intensified by a very sudden temperature change such as occurs in raku. Intensified crackles are possible from raku by placing carbonaceous materials such as burning straw over the cooling pot. All crackle glazes may be intensified in effect by use of a coloring oxide, various other chemicals, inks, or black tea. Crackle networks in the Orient were achieved by successive firings using differing colorants to intensify the crack.

Crackles are most noticeable in white bodies. They are beautiful in light-toned or gray glazes. A pot with crackle is unsuitable for tableware.

Crystalline Glazes

Crystalline glazes are created, for the most part, from two metals. One has large zinc crystal clusters embedded in the glaze. The second, called aventurine, has iron crystals suspended in the glaze that catch and reflect the light. These crystals are flat spangles. Iron and zinc crystals require overloads of at least twenty percent of these metals in the glaze. They usually require fluxes that are highly alkaline and of low atomic weight. Zinc crystals respond best to soda and lithium fluxes. The best crystalline glazes are fritted.

Mattes

Many matte glazes are the result of glazes not heated to a sufficient temperature to become glossy. By this standard, matte effects may be created by lowering the firing temperature or decreasing the flux in a glaze or by increasing the alumina content by kaolin additions. Commercial companies make many excellent frits that mature at Cone 04.

Additions of fifteen percent kaolin give a matte effect. Mattes are also a function of glaze thickness, some glazes being quite glossy when thin but strongly matted upon thicker application.

Several chemicals have a marked effect in producing mattes, partially due to a minor crystalline tendency in the glaze. Good mattes are possible from barium, zinc, titanium, and iron when the glaze is properly compounded and slowly cooled.

Raku

Raku glazes are low-fired glazes used on clay bodies that will withstand the shock of being removed from the kiln while red hot. Often, porous stoneware bodies or bodies with talc may be used.

Raku has deep roots in Zen Buddhism and the Japanese tea ceremonial. Raku pots are known for their quality, and their glaze often makes them art objects. Simple, earthy bowls are common, and collectors often prize even defects. The special firing procedure is part of raku technique. Normally the temperature reached is under 1750°F. The glaze contains low-temperature fluxes that combine with the silica on the pot to form a glaze. Some of the creativity of the raku experience lies in the ability to observe the glaze forming on a red-hot pot and determine when the glaze is sufficiently molten to be finished. One firing I did at Ghost Ranch was especially dramatic because we had the pots on a shuttle (wheel-in) kiln. Successful removal of the pots required the cooperation of at least a dozen persons.

Reduction Glazes

These are glazes produced with a deficiency of oxygen in the kiln atmosphere, creating special effects of color and texture. In reduction, red glazes may be made from a small amount of copper and tin. Celadon glazes result from the reduction of iron colorant, giving subdued green-related tones of color. The ancient wood-burning kilns of the Orient reduced naturally. Present day artist potters usually damper the kiln somewhat to create reduction.

17

TESTING GLAZES

Freedom and intuition must always operate within the context of the essential properties of materials. Such tools as the following are basic:

1. Knowledge of melting point of each ingredient.

2. Knowledge of percent of each ingredient in a batch (chemical analysis helps).

3. Knowledge of how materials react to other materials. This includes awareness of how one flux in combination with others may affect the total batch (eutectics).

4. Knowledge of the specialized functions of materials. For example, those that may induce color, opacity, gloss or matte finish, and crystallization. One material may block the normal function of another.

5. Respect for the interplay of flux, gloss, and matte. For example, if you are trying to build a wood-ash glaze and you get alligator skin, add flux. If the glaze is running, use kaolin. Crystallines and Sang-de-Boeufs which run over the pot may, for good reasons, be low on alumina.

6. Respect for basic rules: exchange only fluxes with other fluxes, clays with clays, and silica amounts with similar silica amounts.

7. Access to a good ceramic library and the discipline to use it.

The following are helpful criteria in designing an in-depth glaze experiment:

1. Statement of objective. A statement of experiences that show the attainment

of the objective or indicate practical precedents and directions for obtaining the objective.

2. List of materials used that point to a theoretical assumption of their functions in the experiment.

3. Statement of known factors that are nonvariable; for example, a given mineral in a glaze is known to contribute best at a given percent.

4. Statement of unknown and variable factors, such as amounts of a given glaze ingredient to be tried.

5. A methodology. Vary only one factor at a time in a given test or trial batch.

Here is an example of the use of the foregoing facts:

1. Objective:
    To attain a Cone 2 Goldstone glaze. (See section on iron crystalline glazes.)
    Precedents:
    (a) One given flux will function better than others. Boron was shown to be a superior activator of Cone 2 iron crystalline glazes.
    (b) An overload of iron oxide is required.

2. Theoretical assumptions of functions of materials needed:
    (a) Silica is needed substantially in order to form glass.
    (b) Alumina must be in small amounts, so feldspathic materials should be limited.
    (c) Simplify the glaze—not more than four ingredients.

3. Known factors: Iron oxide at 20-22% will be regarded as a safe amount of overload.

4. Unknown or variable factors: will emerge during the experiment. Keep careful records.

5. Methodology:
  (a) Fire with an extremely slow cooling to allow time for crystals to grow.
  (b) Lower the temperature and hold it at a point where crystals grow.
  (c) Try the recipe, repeat by increasing in amount all known combinations of three ingredients by twenty percent.

Since I wanted to find a way to test new combinations of glazes containing four components, I devised the four-component system described in the following section on testing.

18

EXAMPLES OF TESTS

Testing glazes can be very creative if one has the urge to discover and a good methodology. One gets the thrill of discovering new glazes, new colors, and new combinations and the adventure of adjusting for glaze defects, adjusting glaze-maturing temperatures, and improving texture.

The materials needed are simple. First, a gram scale and a mortar and pestle or screen. The samples, usually 50 or 100 grams, may be put in plastic cups with lids. The container (with lid held on) is shaken thoroughly to give a good dry mix, which is then blended with enough water to make a paste and ground with a mortar and pestle. If mortar and pestle are not available, add enough water for normal glaze application and screen it. To apply, use a brush at least an inch wide and put on several coats, brushing both up and down and crosswise. When glazed the test piece should be scratched with a nail to verify sufficient thickness. (One percent of bentonite in a glaze is always important to avoid glaze settling, thereby reducing the stirring of the glaze.) The thickness is influenced by both water content of slip and density of the bisque sample glazed.

Test Tile

The test tile has various shapes. Roll out slabs about three-eighth inch thick, then cut the slabs into strips about two to three inches wide and six inches long. Bend the piece off the center about one-half inch so that a right angle is formed. Trim it in the leather state, dry it, and give it a bisque fire. Apply moderately thick glaze on the inside vertical, thinner glaze on the outside vertical, and thick glaze on the horizontal part which is the longest.

Apply thick glaze on the inside length which is longest. Using the unglazed inside for standing vertical in the kiln, apply a moderately thick glaze. Apply a thinner coat on the back of the upright piece.

Make a round shape on the wheel with a cup-like center, flaring out at the top to an almost horizontal angle. Mark the piece with a ceramic marker into sections, somewhat as you cut pie into pieces. Apply glaze to the individual sections, marking on the unglazed area underneath a number designating the glaze's content.

Line Blend

Among the varied ways of testing glazes one of the simplest is the line blend. Let us look at several techniques which are adaptations of the line blend.

1. A potter can run tests with two components of a glaze or with two glazes. There are numerous ways of dividing the glaze into two parts, such as (A) Clay and silica, (B) Fluxes, (C) Color. Tests may be 80% of (A) and 20% of (B), 60% of (A) and 40% of (B), 50% of (A) and 50% of (B), etc. You might have a colorant using 0.5%, 1%, or 1.5%, etc.

2. Another approach to line blending is to add a given percent of each of the ingredients to the glaze. Thus, one might add 5%, 10%, 15%, or whatever one determines of each of the ingredients to 100% of the total. Thus, 100% glaze plus 10% kaolin; 100% glaze plus 15% silica; 100% glaze plus 5% flux; or 100% glaze plus 0.5 to 5% colorant.

3. A similar kind of line blend might look like this:

Base glaze	100	100	100	100	100	100
Additions		4	8	12	16	20
Additions		10	15	20	20	25

(Additives are used for their function.)

4. Under a single variant system, each of the ingredients is varied by a given percentage; for example, 5% to 10%. The potter mixes glaze samples, creating one with a 5% increase in an ingredient and another sample with a 5% decrease. The ideal for this method—actually for all methods—is to vary only one factor at a time. An example of a starting point would be a glaze containing: Spar 20 (40%); Calcium Carbonate 10 (20%); Silica 10 (20%); Dolomite 5 (15%).

Spar might be increased from 40% to 45% or decreased to 35%; other elements might then be altered in the same way.

5. The above single-variant system is ideal for discovering ash glazes. We hold one ingredient (ash content) constant and vary alumina and spar as the glaze needs more or less flux to form a non-flowing fused glass. One might start with 30% ash, 35% spar, and 25% kaolin. Assuming, for example, the glaze needs flux, one could try this line blend:

potash spar	35	40	45	50
kaolin	25	20	15	10
ash	30	10	30	30

This procedure is an easy one because two of the ingredients are known by their function: (1) flux (spar), (2) refractory (kaolin), and (3) body bulk of unknown chemistry (ash). With the ash content constant, the spar and clay are changed in 5% increments.

Triaxial Blend

To test three components, using one glaze or three glazes for example, you might have a triaxis like the one in the accompanying drawing. At the base of the triaxial are three components. The method is very helpful in developing texture, in observing matte versus gloss, and in the discovery of colors. Again, the ash glazes are good for using triaxial tests.

Tri-Axial Diagram
Charting mixtures of Kaolin, Feldspar and Ash for developing an Ash Glaze

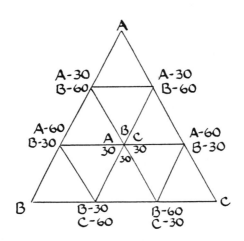

A Four-Component System

I had a mix years ago in Indian Hills, Colorado, that was the Goldstone (aventurine). I wanted a vast crystal field and used the four components listed as A, B, C, D. I listed the amounts of the four components. This is an example of percentages listed:

I.	A	B	C	D
	30	35	20	15
1	+			
2		+		
3			+	
4				+

II.	A	B	C	D
	30	35	20	15
1	+	+		
2	+		+	
3	+			+
4		+	+	+
5		+		+
6			+	+

III.	A	B	C	D
	30	35	20	15
1	+	+	+	
2	+	+		+
3	+		+	+
4		+	+	+

The plus signs may indicate increases of 20% in each single ingredient. For example, 20% of 35 grams equals 7-plus grams, which added to the 35 gives us 42 grams.

The Number I group of pluses represents all of the possible increases of only one component.

The Number II group of pluses represents all the possible increases using increases of two components.

The Number III group lists all of the possible increases of three components. Increases of all four components would not materially affect the recipe.

In all, there were fourteen combinations. After the first firing, one of the combinations showed a marked increase in crystallization. This one was used as a new base of operations. Each new firing repeated the combinations of possible plus increases.

Glaze Shivering or Crazing

If a glaze crazes, there is a problem in the coefficient of thermal expansion. This means that when the fired pot is warmed, the glaze expands more than the clay. The stretched glaze forms small cracks because the glaze is in tension. The opposite situation occurs when the glaze is in compression. A compressed glaze contracts more than the pot does when it cools. Where it is compressed, it pops off the piece. This happens first on the lip.

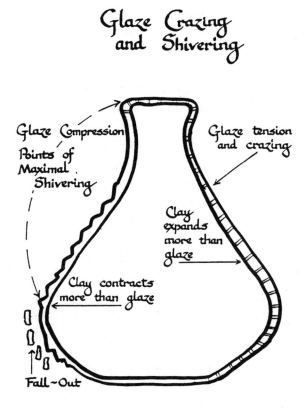

Heat a glazed piece in the oven to 500°. Plunge it in ice water. Repeat several times. Observe if the glaze crazes. Tap the lip with a steel chisel on the raised areas. If glaze pops off, it is compressed.

A potter may proceed with much abandon and freedom, following intuitions about the threefold function of fluxes, glass-forming (silica), and refractoriness (alumina). One might say correctly that a glaze is a scientifically constructed molecule sharing the relation of a monoxide unit to dioxides and trioxides. Yet, a glaze is an agglomeration which, when placed on a pot, will still be a glaze. If it should run, one can stiffen it with alumina. If it is a matte (too dry), one can add flux. If it is a poor color, one can use it inside a pot. All the laws of chemical balance are shattered in such a glaze, but it is still a glaze.

This is the freedom of the potter. Usually chemical balance need not be adjusted to get a glaze. All things melt, given sufficient heat. Absolutely nothing prevents the potter from putting a dash of this or that in a glaze. There is no chemical overlord presiding over the glorious melee of a glaze. Only one thing is necessary: weigh it accurately! To create a non-repeatable glory is a tragedy.

Another example of artistic freedom is how, with intuitive ideas of flux, glass, and refractory function, the potter approaches two materials with divergent chemicals, like these:

	Silica	Alumina	Flux
Sericite Mica	52%	35%	9-10%
Volcanic Ash	72%	12%	9-10%

The potter may, without weighing molecular equivalents, by sheer intuitive guessing, come up with this simplified version of a working glaze:

Sericite Mica	50	Colemanite 30	Kaolin 10	Silica 10
Volcanic Ash	70	Whiting 20	Kaolin 10	Silica 0

Both of the above are working glazes, but the potter, looking at the high alumina content of the mica, low in silica, proceeds to add silica and colemanite as a powerful flux to attack the refractory alumina.

The potter, using freedom and intuition, will notice all kinds of reactions at work that will make a glaze what it is. Keep your pencil sharp and notebook handy.

PART VI:

SANG-DE-BOEUF

GLAZE

19

HISTORIC PINNACLE

The Sang-de-Boeuf glaze (Chinese oxblood) stands alone among historic ceramic glazes. It represents the pinnacle of three thousand years of Chinese history. To own an oxblood is an unparalleled joy to the collector, and to make one is the contemporary potter's dream.

The secrets of deep tonality and texture, untarnished by maroon and scarlet yet hovering between the two, have been shrouded in mystery. Whether contemporary potters or ancient Chinese potters, those filling the kiln with glazed pots must feel themselves on an abyss of foreboding. Long labors are necessary to produce this glaze, and the mistress behind the curtain does not easily unveil her secrets. Some may shrug their shoulders, saying they prefer some other color—blue perhaps—yet the fact remains that there is a deep pulsebeat for this glaze, an instinctual response, an irrepressible passion. Many who see a great oxblood will never again settle for peach or plum.

The Chinese succeeded through the line of tradition. Guidelines for contemporary potters have to be sifted out. In general, potters have failed at Sang-de-Boeuf, and very few produce in successful quantity. The reasons for this may now be better understood. Chinese potters were among the most gifted, and their work is the very best. The "red epoch" seems to be the culmination of a three thousand-year historical period. To understand this glaze, unravel its mystery, and see its place in ceramic history is a thrill. The difficulties of the search only increase the satisfactions of discovery.

The dearth of historical material increases the problem. Illumination from the past is dim, but an occasional elusive beam of light is shown. More is to be learned from further excavations of pottery sites.

Spiritual hunger fathered this glaze through its infancy. It was first mentioned in the fifteenth century, and a sixteenth-century manuscript describes eleven different specimens with colored drawings. Limited in quantity, it was called "sacrificial red." Hsiang Yuan-Pien states in his manuscript, "It is truly the very crown of our collections of celebrated porcelain of different dynasties...the tint of the red is crimson like fresh blood...of the tone of ripe red cherries, or rather, like the precious stones brought by the turbaned red-socked nomads from the west."[23]

Although we have no specimen of this red, there is little doubt, according to one authority, that it was a copper-red under a feldspathic glaze produced at a high temperature.[24]

During the reign of K'ang Hse (1662-1722), Ching Dynasty, the Sang-de-Boeuf (also called the Lang Yao) copper-red was made. It was similar to the sacrificial red described by Hsiang Yuan-Pien. This glaze was gradually perfected and produced in a variety of places, but eventually declined in quality and production. The original quality was lost and never recovered by Chinese potters. [25]

20

PROBLEMS

Our purpose is to study red glazes produced from copper colorants at high temperature (Cone 10 range) by means of oxygen deficiency in the kiln. Many of the attempts to get reds fail. There are good reds, mule-liver reds, and oxidized gray-greens. Some despair of ever knowing what the decisive factors are in forming red glazes.

The failure of most potters to get reds or to produce in successful quantity can be attributed to several factors:

1. Many have tried to produce reds by recipe, reduction, or both, not knowing the relative requirements and needs of both.

2. Few experimental approaches were adequate to give results easily interpreted. For example, few have used several sets of recipes in the same section of the kiln. When they have, they have often repeated firings, hoping to get similar results, when in an additional firing the same atmospheric conditions were not present. Many use controls inappropriately: stringent controls are either lacking or not easily attainable.

3. There has been no clearcut answer to the question of what temperatures are best for reduction and for how long the reduction is needed.

4. The amount of reduction has either not been known or has not been measurable by clearcut means in the kiln operation.

5. Reds have been produced both with and without an oxidation period at the end of the firing. Factors in this have not been understood. This is a most basic discrepancy we shall try to resolve.

6. Differences in kilns require differing applications of reduction. A downdraft kiln, or one with a small combustion chamber, may reduce very easily. A dynamic updraft kiln with excellent combustion conditions may require a stronger and more consistent reduction of oxygen. The former kilns, reducing easily, may tolerate oxidation at the finish, whereas the latter may not.

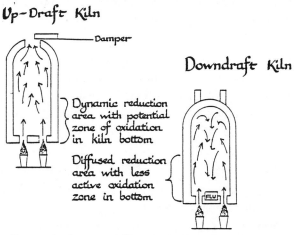

Up-Draft Kiln

Damper

Downdraft Kiln

Dynamic reduction area with potential zone of oxidation in kiln bottom

Diffused reduction area with less active oxidation zone in bottom

FLUE

Down-draft kiln diffuses reduction through entire kiln.

Up-draft kiln tends to oxidize near floor.

21

CHEMICAL APPROACH

During the 1930s, ceramic engineers showed much interest in the study of Sang-de-Boeuf. I have reviewed some of the factors at work in the glaze from a standpoint of the chemistry involved.

All of the metals unite with oxygen to form oxides. Most of the early Chinese glazes used iron and copper for colorants, reducing them in a natural state of oxygen deficiency. Let us look at the chemical reaction of copper. Some elements, such as copper, have more than one valence. Following are some chemical valences at work:

	Less Oxygen		More Oxygen	
Copper	Cuprous oxide	Cu_2O	Cupric oxide	CuO
Iron	Ferrous oxide	FeO	Ferric oxide	Fe_2O_3
Tin	Stannous oxide	SnO	Stannic oxide	SnO_2

These elements may have other valences. The suffix "ous" is used where the element has a lower positive value, which in such cases signifies less oxygen.

22

THE ROLE OF TIN OXIDE

The role of tin oxide in the copper reds is complex. In his classic memoir DIE ROTEN AND GEFLAMMTEN KUPFEROXYDULGLASUREN, Dr. H.A. Seger gives us this account of an experiment:

"When cupric oxide is heated in a glaze to 400 and 500 degrees C in a reducing atmosphere, there remain metallic copper and sintered glaze. If heated again to 950 degrees, it forms a gray frit. If powdered and mixed with 1% of tin oxide, it furnishes a beautiful red glaze first."[26]

Dr. Seger intentionally adds that the glaze is melted in air as the oxidizing agent converts metallic copper into cuprous oxide. The role of this oxygen will be discussed.

"It is doubtful if these auxiliary oxides of tin and iron are essential for the development of the copper red, but H.A. Seger...and others are agreed that the production of the better type of copper red is greatly facilitated."[27]

Cupric and stannic oxide are first of all reduced simultaneously to cuprous and stannous oxides. This is followed by the localized reduction of cuprous oxide by stannous oxide. The hunger of stannous oxide for oxygen apparently robs and reduces the oxygen remaining in the copper. Chemists feel that tin oxide's role in dispersing, stabilizing, and maintaining the red color is not easily explainable. The grain size of copper, relating to the red factor, is something in which tin also has a role. The dual role of tin and its effect on grain size implies that stannic as well as stannous oxide affects the glaze. This dual process may be what gives the red glaze its brightness and intensity, noted when the glaze is fluid enough to move down on the piece and coalesce into red brilliance.

Normal oxidizing heat turns cupric oxide into a finely divided state that is colloidal. A colloid, in contrast to a crystalloid, is a jelly-like substance that will not pass through a membrane. It has been estimated that the diameter of minute and ultramicroscopic particles is about ten microns, or 0.025 inch. The color reaction of copper oxides is related directly to their grain size.

Chemists have generally felt that, as reduction increases, the grain size of copper increases. Also, the various colors in the five layers to be noted in the next chapter seem to fit the picture we would get from looking at the various grain sizes of copper. Stannic oxide may help to maintain and stabilize the colloidal state. Then again, it could help disperse the colloidal copper into a red film.

23

THE FIVE-LAYER FACT

Of tremendous interest in all this is the appearance of apparent layers when a Chinese red is magnified one hundred times by the electron microscope. Spectroscope analysis, incidentally, tells us the chemicals in the glazes. Passing downward from the surface of the glaze, one sees a kind of rainbow band with the sequence of yellow, red, and blue. These three colors are preceded and followed by a more or less transparent glaze, making five layers in all. The upper layer is oxidized and the lower one reduced.

Let us look at these layers, in order, from the surface of the glaze:

1. Colorless Layer
This is a cupric, oxidized glaze, very faintly green due to the small amount of copper (usually under one-half of one percent).

2. Yellow Layer
This is a narrow band of color from colloidal copper in a very fine state of division. It has been called an arrested stage in the oxidation of the copper color, a transitional stage between the red layer underneath and the pale green above. The red film is reduced in size, and appears yellow before it vanishes.

3. Red Layer
This is cuprous oxide in a less finely divided state than the yellow.

4. Blue Layer
A narrow band.

5. Colorless Layer
This may be copper metal or cuprous oxide produced by reduction. It is a derivative of red over-reduced. It has, with oxidation following reduction, the

potential of becoming blue and subsequently red. The colorless particles, extremely small, appear under transmitted light to be blue.

The five-layer idea, explained fully by J.W. Mellor of the Mellor Laboratories, Stoke on Trent, was attested to by a substantial group of engineers who collaborated and studied the matter prior to 1940. There is a possibility the copper glazes are reduced to five or more colors depending upon the stage of reduction.[28]

This multicolor glaze may be expressed as follows in terms of degrees of oxidation:

High oxidation	pale blue or green
Decreased	faint yellow-red tinge
Reduction	red
More reduction	blue
Still more reduction	pale gray or green
Extreme	dark or metallic

24

THE SEQUENTIAL THEORY

The sequential theory is that reds are best obtained by one reduction period followed by one oxidation period. This should not be confused with additional alternations of reduction and oxidation. The concept proposed by Dr. Mellor is that a glaze is first reduced and then oxidized. This time sequence suggests the reduction phase first and the oxidation phase second, the former being a kind of initiator and the latter accounting for the final redness. It is assumed that the first stage in the reduction process is the reduction by hydrocarbons of the cupric and stannic oxide to cuprous and stannous oxides.

Dr. A.L. Hetherington notes that, "The copper-red glazes have been looked upon as the result of a reducing atmosphere only. Now that Dr. Mellor has established the role played by aerial oxygen as a finish to reducing action, many of the variations of reduced copper glaze become more intelligible."[29]

He corroborates the notion of Dr. Mellor that reds are a reduction/oxidation sequential phenomenon: "The copper-red glaze is brought about by a reducing atmosphere at the outset and it is finished off in an oxidizing atmosphere."[30]

Dr. Mellor emphasizes also that the process of one layer oxidizing the layer underneath it is the final—and vital—process in acquiring the red.

"The red is derived from the (lower) colorless zone, and the upper colorless zone from the red band. The presence of the upper colorless zone demonstrates the permeability of the glaze to aerial oxygen...."[31]

"A greenish almost colorless layer next to the body probably contains copper or cuprous oxide in solution and under the right conditions it forms rouge flambe."[32]

We noted in the previous quotation from Dr. Seger's experiment and his comments on use of tin that he first creates metallic copper and sintered glaze. This suggests extreme reduction. It would seem that augmented oxygen would be required to convert metallic copper to cuprous oxide. This experiment may have furthered the idea of Dr. Mellor's mistaken sequential notion.

It is obvious that in proportion to the extent of extreme reduction, an oxidation period is required. This is to say that the oxidation is a compensatory factor to over-reduction. It will be noted later that some kiln practices discredit the need for sequential firing.

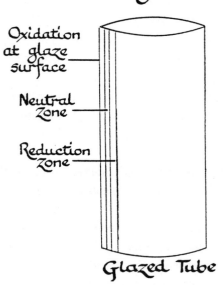

Glazed Tube

In Kiln practice we deal with three layers.

25

THEORY VERSUS KILN PRACTICE

The sprung arch downdraft kiln gives good reds consistently without an oxidation period. In the kiln I currently use, a dynamic updraft kiln made by the West Coast Kiln Company, I have never used an oxidation cycle.

The kiln operated at the Ghost Ranch Conference Center near Abiquiu, New Mexico, by James Kempes and me has never used an oxidation period. In fact, the opposite of this augmented reduction by clouds of smoke just prior to the kiln turn-off did not hinder (nor help) reds. The Ranch reds have been noted as consistently good over a ten-year period.

Other Potters Not Reporting An Oxidation Cycle

George Wettlaufer, ceramic engineer and potter, starts fairly heavy reduction at Cone 06 (about 1850°F or less) for 45 minutes. This registers 9.15 on his carbon dioxide (CO_2) indicator. After this he reduces at point eleven on the indicator, turning off the kiln at Cone 10 with no mention of an oxidizing period at Cone 10.[33]

Carlton Ball usually fires a continuous reduction starting at 1400-1600°F. A flame of two to three inches at the bottom peephole indicates to him reduction is correct. His kiln is the same as the updraft West Coast kiln at Ghost Ranch, and he reports no difference in using other updraft kilns. He writes:

"The updraught kilns oxidize as they cool. Downdraught kilns sometimes require a different procedure. If a downdraught kiln is closed tightly around the burner ports after shut-off, the kiln may not oxidize much as it cools. This would make a difference in the final effect."[34]

Joseph Grebanier, with painstaking methods, recommends a kiln cycle remarkable for its insight:

1. Moderate reduction initiated at about 1425°F, followed by a fuller degree of reduction at 1650°.

2. At 1875°, as in the case of his Chun pots, the fullest possible reduction is continued for three-quarters of an hour.

3. After the heavy reduction for three-quarters of an hour, the reduction is gradually lessened, and in the final hour he shows only the slightest possible quantity of flame at the stack. He calls it near-neutral, but it is still reduction until the kiln is turned off at Cone 9. [35]

Potters Using Oxidation

Harding Black of San Antonio fired reds successfully for many years and wrote me as follows: "My reduction firing as of now is to start reduction when I can see color in the kiln, reduce until Cone 6 is down, then oxidize until Cone 10 is down." [36]

The Reverend Mr. Kring of New York City reports success using an oxidation period at the finish. The type of kiln used is not clear to me, but it was fired by forced air burners.

In conclusion, heavy reduction periods, or kilns that by nature reduce heavily, do tolerate an oxidation cycle for compensation. The words of James Kempes of Ghost Ranch, relative to an oxidation period, were "Never, it's suicide to reds." [37]

The evidence of the Chinese Naboro-Gami kilns appears conclusive. There was no way they could provide an oxidation period in any kilns other than those at the top of the hill, which were last turned off.

26

KILN OPERATION IN COPPER REDS

There are no photographs of the layers present in the studio potters' red pots as there are in spectroscopic analysis of the old Sang-de-Boeuf. Lacking the same cycle the Chinese used, there may be variance in the layers. In kiln firing it appears sufficient to know we are dealing with three basic layers or zones: the upper oxidized, the intermediate zone of colloidal copper, and the lower reduced zone.

In the finished pot, we have noted a light blue or green which may indicate oxidation. A darkened red "liver color" or red intertwined with purple, heavy blue-purple, or red purple may indicate heavy reduction has taken over.

Use of Damper and Peephole

As one partially closes the kiln damper, pressure is exerted on the gases in the kiln, which are forced out of the peepholes, causing a reduction atmosphere. Closing the burner at the point of intake of primary air also achieves reduction, but if done by means of the damper alone, reduction is more easily measured. Likewise, reduction is more easily discernible by indication at the peephole when the damper alone is used to effect reduction.

If the appearance of the inside of the kiln is somewhat murky or cloudy rather than clear, we assume that reduction is taking place. In reduction, the flames at the burner port will become sluggish and will spill out of the port in extreme reduction. As reduction is increased, the length of the flame shooting out the peephole will be longer and smokier and its color may be an intense yellow.

Another problem from observing reduction at the peephole is that the flame is very difficult to see if it is in bright sunlight. If one can create artificial shade, or fire in the evening or on a cloudy day, it is much easier.

Another indication of reduction is flame at the damper. This indicates unburned fuel has traveled all the way through the kiln chamber. Black smoke at the damper and elsewhere indicates unburned fuel. Since only carbon monoxide and not free carbon enters into the reduction process, smoke indicates fuel waste and air pollution without practical benefits from reduction.

Since one may reduce without seeing flame, there is a surer method of detection. If a sliver of wood is placed in the spy-hole, it will burn or smoke. If the flame or smoke is moving out of the peephole, the kiln is reducing. If the splinter burns and the flame is moving into the kiln, the kiln is oxidizing. This movement of smoke into the kiln should usually be avoided, although a neutral direction is tolerable for a time.

A short flame coming out of the peephole, with or without the stick, is usually sufficient indication of reduction for copper red. However, if the flame and smoke come out of one peephole and not another, which often happens in the peephole nearer the kiln floor, one may need to increase the vigor of flame at one peephole in order to create it at the other. If the atmosphere appears rather clear in the peephole not showing flame, then some egressive flame may be needed. In the peephole showing most flame there is a tolerable variance. That is, we may operate for a short period without seeing flame or with a longer somewhat smoky flame without too much risk.

Reduction Indications

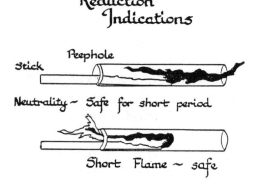

Stick • Peephole

Neutrality ~ Safe for short period

Short Flame ~ safe

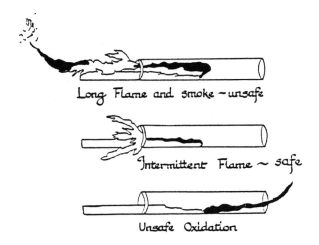

Long Flame and smoke ~ unsafe

Intermittent Flame ~ safe

Unsafe Oxidation

Use of Indicator

One may use a carbon dioxide (CO_2) indicator to measure the amount of reduction, or oxidation for that matter. The cumulative evidence of good reds produced by the kiln can be related to the CO_2 indicated in the firings. The CO_2 indicator shows numerically the amount of oxidation or reduction and also the area of maximal combustion efficiency, which is without excess carbon or oxygen, namely, a neutral atmosphere. A high number on the scale—a hypothetical 15, for example—indicates no excess of carbon or oxygen. As the number drops, the CO_2 count is decreased and reduction is measured.

It should be noted that the primary help from an indicator is that it gives objective results from a given kiln. These results may be applied to another kiln with caution until substantiated by the resultant colors. Many potters prefer not to use such a scientific method; they simply observe the atmosphere in the kiln or the peephole. Since the peephole flame is hard to see, and because of the need for minimal reduction, the method of observing the burning stick is the best starting point.

In the kiln operation there should be a period of slow kiln advance of less than 100 degrees per hour for the last hour. This will give better glazes, and this slow period will survive satisfactorily a moderate increase in reduction.

Oxidation and Temperature Advance

The risk in most kilns is oxidation at the finish of the fire, or oxidation from the cooling cycle. An updraft kiln is more responsive to a quick flow and exit of oxygen. Some kilns, like the downdraft, permit more easily some oxidation before the turn-off.

One needs to consider the relation of reduction to temperature advance and evenness of temperature. There is an increase of heat with less fuel when oxygen is increased. The heat advance will be slowed with increased reduction. This in turn may require more fuel. Increased reduction may make it very difficult to keep from losing heat in the top of the kiln. Given these factors, one may need to increase oxygen in the kiln. This can be done with only a slight peephole flame appearing. There is a delicate balance at work bordering on a need for a brief neutral atmosphere. A moderated reduction to give heat advance will not hurt the desired glaze effect.

Maintaining correct reduction may be a delicate operation of moving the damper only one-fourth inch or less. This is an operation that takes patience. Cones may become invisible in a reduced, murky atmosphere. A momentary opening of the damper will show the cones, and it will not hurt the glazes. If the cones are slow in appearing, a little more time is permissible.

A kiln with open spaces between pots invites oxidation and uneven temperature. A uniform tight pack gives uniformity to reds. Whenever there is some air intake during cooling, such as proximity to combustion areas, one may expect light-colored pots instead of reds.

Open burner ports are permissible when cooling if the damper is tight. If there is a way to close burner ports during cooling, the danger of oxidation is lessened. One can open the damper some only after red heat is gone, at 900 to 1100°F.

27

WHEN TO REDUCE

Starting Point

Since reduction is best done in the heat cycle, let us repeat the information on the starting point for a Cone 10 glaze. Under 1400°F, carbon is not actively released to form CO_2. Under about 1525°F, the carbons deposited in the ware may fill the pores and cause bloating or bubbling of the body and pinholing and pitting in the glaze.

While bodies do not actually oxidize, they do absorb carbons in the pores which are not easily released when the body matures and the pores close. Satisfactory reds may be made by starting reduction under 1550°F; however, 1600° is a good place to start. Also, it is best to start under 1700° because of the advantage of a longer heat cycle for reduction. Reduction at this temperature is good because there is less hydrogen in the gases: hydrogen hinders good reds.

Reduction continues without interruption until the kiln is turned off. A steady pattern without variance of intensity, as we have noted, works well. If the steady pattern is to be varied, it should be done as in the aforementioned practice of Joseph Grebanier, who intensifies reduction, starting at 1875°F, when the glaze is entering its liquid phase.

28

LANDMARKS OF CERTAINTY

These are the basic certainties:

1. To get good reds, copper and tin must be used. Copper oxide—one-half of one percent and less—and tin oxide under two percent are usually sufficient. Tin assists in reduction.

2. A wide variety of fluxes in recipes will work. Sodium and potassium from feldspars, calcium, boron, and lithium work well.

3. Apparently, the red glaze is in reality a layer of five colors, although in practice we may work successfully assuming only three layers.

4. A good range for starting high-temperature reduction is 1500-1700°F, continued until the heat is off.

5. Reduction can be determined by a CO_2 indicator or by placing sticks in the peephole to determine if smoke or flame is being drawn into the kiln or being expelled. The latter method is very reliable.

6. Re-oxidation after kiln turn-off can be avoided by tightly closing the damper and plugging burner ports if need be. A tightly-packed kiln and a downdraft type kiln may help prevent re-oxidation.

7. The grain size of copper is decreased as red color is reached.

8. Sequential firing—that is, oxidizing after reducing—is unnecessary in most kiln experiences. A very moderate but long-sustained reduction period (starting at 1600°F) eliminates the need for sequential firing. This experience holds true in both small, modern kilns and the large, Chinese Naboro-Gami kilns.

PART VII:

SPECIAL

GLAZE

ADVENTURES

29

THE IRON STORY

No chemical compares with iron oxide in the variety of rich effects possible. It exceeds all other metals, including copper. Iron responds to new and old chemicals with bewildering richness, providing new colors. The next chapter, "Crystalline Glazes," describes my Cone 10 Aventurine and Cone 02 and Cone 2 Aventurines, each with iron crystals.

Other than the aventurines, when we deal with iron we are dealing with subtlety. The celadons are not garish. They are a muted tonality of blue, green, and gray. The Temmoku family has rich variants but always in the subdued tones of black and brown.

Artists creating iron glazes usually have a taste for subtlety which leaves them uninterested in the bright intensity of copper reds, blues, and greens. They talk of red, yellow, and orange, but these are often muted to the point of barely qualifying as such. The possibilities of muted color and texture are infinite, and they follow the whole span of the color wheel.

In general we may classify the iron glazes into five groups:

1. The celadon (reduced) are in the gray, blue, green area.

2. The Temmoku are black and brown, produced by incipient crystallization and other factors.

3. Related to Temmoku are the special brown-black configurations, such as hare's fur, partridge feather, oil spot, khaki, and alligator skin, which are often produced by the bubbling process.

4. Special varieties too numerous to mention give color ranges such as plum red, dull orange, and yellow.

5. Aventurine (Goldstone) glazes are produced by an overload of iron and use as much as twice the amount found in Temmoku glazes.

There are reasons for giving space to "the Iron Family" rather than furthering the much-covered writing on colors derived from other oxides. The iron colors offer unique possibilities for new discoveries through experimentation, and they build on the great Chinese classical traditions from the copper and iron metals and their reduction. The celadons are reduced. The Temmoku family in some cases comprise both oxidation and reduction glaze. For the most part, celadons are more easily produced than the Sang-de-Boeuf.

The Celadons

There are two chief oxides of iron, ferrous oxide (FeO) and ferric oxide (Fe_2O_3). The ferrous, having less iron, is in the reduced state. Celadon colors range from gray to light green, blue-green, pale blue, and olive green. The color variants of celadons are due to several factors, including the amount of iron, the temperature, and the extent of reduction. A small degree of reduction may give an olive tone to the green. Also, the chemicals used affect color. Alkaline glazes differ from those in which the acids dominate. Blue and green in celadons are due to constituents of the glaze, although firing conditions are also a factor.

I get a blue celadon from a glaze using feldspar and whiting, and a greenish tone from one using lithium. Many subtle factors are at work. The Sung potters worked with both reduced and oxidized iron. Their celadons were gloriously translucent and without equal.

Those who appreciate softness and subtlety appreciate celadons. The modern potter's best chances are from ball-milled glazes, scrupulously applied, with enough depth in application for richness. Although some celadons are opaque, the best ones are not, and they show all the little scars and working of the clay body. Scrupulous sponging of the body to smooth it is required. The faintest underglaze colors show under the celadons. With their translucence they offer a unique possibility of showing body textures underneath. Underglaze effects are strong. Some of the best underglaze colors for celadons are black and bright colors. Any good black recipe for decoration will work.

Mixtures of iron slips with a little cobalt or the usual complex mixes are good. If one has a dependable Sang-de-Boeuf, it can be used; however, if the red fails, all is lost. Decoration of green ware is much preferable to decoration of bisque, although the copper red as colorant spot should go on the bisque.

The many published recipes give details as to effect. The effects vary, and one should try several to know. The following two recipes illustrate basic differences of two colors:

Green Celadon		Blue Celadon (Grebonier)	
Lithium Carbonate	8	Feldspar	83
Whiting	16	Whiting	9
Kaolin	21	Silica	8
Silica	55	Black Iron	1.5
Red Iron Oxide	2		

The Temmoku Family

The Temmoku glaze is really an extended family that includes the varied textural configurations such as hare's fur, tea dust, oil spot, and alligator skin. The wide variety of effects have contributed to lack of authentic definitions.

In this family of iron glazes, we find a rich mirror-black and also black with brown tones in varying shades. The textures vary as the names indicate. An underfired piece may be a "lizard" or "alligator skin." Fired higher, the textural effects increase, due in part to flow of the glaze from increased liquidity. Many other factors contributing to texture and color are found.

Temmoku glazes were first used in Japan on the tea bowls of the Zen monks who inhabited a monastery in the mountains of the Chechiang province Tien-mu-Shan. Called "the mountain of the Eye of Heaven," Temmoku was named after Tien-mu-Shan. From a monastery on this mountain, Dogen, a priest, was said to have brought the first Temmoku bowl to Japan in 1228. Temmoku is actually the Japanese name for Chien ware, often called Chien-yao, produced at Chien-Yang in the Fukien Province. Here the Temmoku reached the pinnacle of development by Sung potters, the unsurpassed makers of all past or present developments from iron.[38]

They developed high-temperature feldspathic glazes, more viscous than previous glazes. Applied thickly, these glazes flowed down the piece in thick rolls, ending just short of the foot. Sung pots included all the textured varieties.

What are the factors at work giving these glazes their varied configurations and tonal dominances? The answers are interesting. A degree of knowledge is needed in order for us to experiment.

First is the general fact that in alkaline glazes, ferric oxide goes into solution more readily than it does in acidic glazes. As the iron goes into solution more, the colors move in the spectrum from black to brown.

Dr. Hetherington tells of a glass-bead experiment in which the glass was filled with both alkaline and acidic chemicals. Ferric oxide was added to the glaze. As the alkali was removed and replaced by acidic material, the iron resisted the solution totally. With increasing alkalies, the iron dissolved and the color became less black, passing through a brown to a brownish-yellow color.[39]

In the Tang dynasty, highly alkaline glazes were used, and the colors varied from rich brown to a light yellow. In the Sung pots, more acidic deep browns and black glazes were the rule.

It is incorrect to refer to the Temmoku family of glazes as basically crystalline glazes. Some effects are produced by bubbling, some are produced by incipient crystals which are immature. These incipient crystals are also seen as they bleed or liquefy, losing structure but leaving their beautiful patterned tonal imprint. The true crystal is a gold spangle of the flaky type seen in the aventurine with an overload of iron. Incipient crystals are seen in many of the Temmoku pots if they have enough iron. Often the free iron introduced supplements iron in the ferruginous clay, and we often do not know the amount.

It would appear that the best chances of configurational pattern from incipient crystallization would require a total iron content of ten percent or more. The crystallization would be improved with silica. Glazes high in boron and sodium would lighten color.

The patterns observable are affected not only by the amount of iron present but by the speed of the cooling process. As in the aventurine, a slow cool gives greater opportunity for crystals to start forming. The glaze may appear to be a cloudy mass of microscopic particles or to have definite crystal outlines. They may have some of the highly reflecting plates of the true aventurine, or they may take feathery, spindly forms as they begin to flow downward on the pot. The crystals may exhibit some of the red from the aventurine gold spangle, which leaves red tones as it bleeds.

Many textures are a result of the bubbling process, and some come from a combination of bubbling and incipient crystallization. Under the microscope, these glazes as they approach crystals show a red figured shape. On a white porcelain they give a beautiful contrast. Of the alkalies, soda is preferable. As a glaze is heated to high temperature, some of the alkali may be volatilized. This alkaline loss has a deleterious effect on color lightness, leaving a blacker tone. The loss may hinder the pattern as well as the color of the pot. If the pot is fired too high or too long, every tonality is blended to a meaningless mesh. There are risks in overfiring from the dissociation of iron. Too much reduction is unwise. A slow cool is preferable.

The bubble-bursting process accounts for much of the "oil spot" glaze. The spots are caused by light reflected from the flat surfaces of the small iron crystals. The analogy of soapsuds in a basin of water helps us to understand the bubble-bursting phenomenon in the glaze. As the suds subside, they leave an even and flat surface on the water, with a filmy deposit of small rings. Bubbles of gas bursting in a glaze leave similar circles, forming pits which are then filled with a more fluid part of the glaze. The material filling the pit, flowing at a different rate than the matrix of the glaze, is also different in color from the matrix.

With the help of magnification, one can see that the surface of the pit-filled glaze retains a bumpy character, with the pit edges only partially smoothed over. Each pit may reveal gray metallic streaks radiating outward. As the glaze is heated higher and the glaze smoothes and liquefies further, the traces of the oil spots will disappear entirely.

So the varied tonal appearance of the Temmoku glazes is due to crystals or bubbles forming and, most likely, a combination of both. These factors help us to formulate ideas for further experimentation with glazes in the Temmoku family.

The content of the Temmoku glazes intimates that the Chinese used iron-bearing stones or slips. Certainly they must have had the experience of overfired earthenware red clay turning into a glaze at high temperature. From this experience there may have followed further experimentation using clay to make slip glazes. Essentially the glazes were high-fired stoneware with an earthenware glaze.

Some excellent Temmoku glazes may be made today with glazes using Albany slip. This slip forms a glaze at Cone 10. Additions to it provide a rich base for experimentation. Five to ten percent rutile added to Albany will give an excellent hare's fur glaze. Yellow ochre, burnt umber, and burnt sienna (all derivatives of iron) may be added to Albany slip with a small amount of lepidolite. About ten percent of the former and five percent of the lepidolite will give oil spot glazes.

These additives with Albany of ten percent iron slips give variants of the Temmoku spectrum. Additives of kaolin will give alligator skin. Additives of soda feldspar or nepheline syenite can produce hare's fur and partridge feather effects. One should experiment with additions of ten to twenty percent.

The Japanese have a Temmoku similar to one hundred parts of Albany and twenty parts by weight of red iron oxide. One may experiment by adding to this twenty parts by weight of various common wood ashes. There are many standard recipes for various Temmoku effects. Some not using slip seem to work equally well. A reliable Cone 10 "oil spot" follows:

Potash Feldspar 45

Whiting	13
China Clay	11
Silica	28
Red Iron Oxide	8

This glaze with thick and thin applications is a rich brown-black medley.

Sandra Simon's Temmoku glaze recipe:[40]

Whiting	17.4
Zinc	2.2
Potash Feldspar	46.4
Kaolin	10.8
Flint	23.2
Iron	0.1

Tom Coleman's Iron Spot Black (Cone 9-10, apply thick):[41]

Potash Feldspar	78
Whiting	6
Silica	14
Red Iron Oxide	7

Some of the most exciting iron glazes incorporate phosphorus. I am intrigued by the subdued red tones in a brown background in this glaze. The effect appears to be from crystallization. Some of the recipes follow:

Cone 9

Albany Slip	52
Nepheline Syenite	25.5
Iron Phosphate	17.5
Dolomite	5

Since iron phosphate is hard to come by, I developed a glaze using bone ash as a source of phosphorus:

Potash Feldspar	17
Whiting	6
Kaolin	3.5
Silica	15
Albany Slip	25
Nepheline Syenite	12
Dolomite	23
Iron Oxide	13
Bone Ash	8

The following recipe, known as Texas Red, is really Mason's Red:

Custer Feldspar	56
Dolomite	8.5
Red Iron Oxide	7
Bone Ash	15.5
Ball Clay	5
Silica	8

The above works in reduction and should be tried in oxidation also. It could conceivably make Goldstone crystals by increasing the iron, at the expense of dolomite, up to 16%. In this case, soda spar could be tried in reduced amounts for luster. Some get better results in this glaze than others. Reducing conditions and thickness of the glaze are determining factors.

The amazing factor in the bone-ash glaze is that good effects can come from using the bone in larger amounts and the iron in smaller amounts. Effects are sometimes good when the reverse is true, when the iron content is above 10 and the ash content is less.

The so-called color spectrum, about which little is known, follows: it should be remembered that iron colors of this sort are muted.

Orange

Custer Feldspar	16
Dolomite	11
Barium Carbonate	11
Edgar Kaolin	7.5
Silica	4.5
Rutile	7.5
Red Iron	2.25

Orange (A strong-colored glaze)

Nepheline Syenite	12
Custer Feldspar	38
Whiting	10
China Clay	7
Titanium Dioxide	6
Barium Carbonate	23

Red

Potash Feldspar	42
Whiting	14
EPK Clay	9
Flint	36
Red Iron Oxide	10

Plum

Cornwall Stone	25
Albany Slip	55
Red Iron Oxide	11
Whiting	10

Textured Tan (Spence)

Custer Spar	30
Barium Carbonate	22
Dolomite	18
Silica	8
China Clay	8
Whiting	5
Zinc Oxide	2
Iron Oxide	3

The tan glaze loses its textural effect as we advance slightly above Cone 10. Variants in iron content should be of interest.

Following are the well-known and much-used Shaner glazes:

Red		Yellow	
Custer Feldspar	46	F 4 Spar	32.5
Whiting	19	Barium Carbonate	25.3
Talc	3.6	Dolomite	12.2
Kaolin	22	Ball Clay	7.2
Bone Ash	9	Ziropax or Superpax	15
Red Iron	3.6	Iron Oxide	2
		Silica	7.2

Try both thick and thin applications. The Shaner glazes show again the amazing versatility of iron used in small amounts. When alumina and phosphorous are used in the Shaner glaze, it is red-like. To bring out the yellow tendency, use a small amount of iron, tinged with barium and a zirconium compound. Such factors in iron give us a new perspective on this "impurity" with its dirty and rusty connotations.

The Temmoku style offers possibilities for decorative effects. The Chinese designed figured Temmoku bowls, decorated with floral or geometric patterns or representations of birds and insects. The figures were most often black on a brown background, though lighter colors on dark backgrounds were also used. All was produced in one firing.

The potter coated the bowl with a glaze mixture known to produce a brown on firing. The desired design was produced by removing the glaze with a pointed and beveled stick. In the vacant area, the right amount of ferric oxide was applied to give a black on firing. The lines where the design was darker or lighter were somewhat blurred rather than sharp, which contributed to the aesthetic interest.

30

CRYSTALLINE GLAZES

The Crystal Forming Process

Historical accounts do not confirm the existence of large zinc crystals in Chinese antiquity, as some have postulated. There were crystals from iron oxide, but they were not the spectacular flaky, gold spangles produced by an overload of iron which we see in contemporary times. The Chinese were making only minute iron crystals centuries ago.

The Rookwood Pottery in Ohio, which showed iron crystal glazes at the 1893 World's Fair, was unsurpassed at iron crystallization. The technique of zinc glaze crystals was seen at exhibitions in Paris, Brussels, and Stockholm in 1897, produced by the French National Factory at Sevres and the royal factories at Copenhagen and Stockholm.

Dr. Ebelman, a noted ceramic engineer, made a study of crystallization from 1847 to 1852. Messrs. Lauth and Dutailly presented papers to the Museum of the National Factory at Sevres in September 1895.

In TRANSACTIONS OF THE AMERICAN CERAMIC SOCIETY, 1903, Dr. Ray Stull wrote, "No portion of the ceramic field is more inviting to experimentation than that of crystal glazes....(N)o branch of glaze making is so capable of giving startling results."[42]

The following observations can be made about the crystallization process:

1. Crystallization in nature is a function of the cooling process. Quartz crystallizes into rare geometric designs. Glass in many forms shows a crystallizing tendency. Water from the sky forms crystal designs as snow flakes. Jack Frost on a window pane shows a form of crystallized water.

2. For our purposes, iron and zinc are the chemicals yielding the best results. They react to the silica by forming beautiful crystals. Iron forms a plate-like spangle reflecting tones of gold, and the crystal is red as it melts. Zinc forms rare patterns and sizes; some zinc crystals resemble flowers. Coloration is easy to achieve in zinc crystals; the usual metal oxides bring color.

3. The iron and zinc must be introduced as "overloads," often representing twenty percent or more parts by weight of the glaze.

4. Chemists compare the glaze to a solution of salt in water in which the excessive amount is precipitated out. Similar to salt, the iron and zinc particles, being excess, cannot be dissolved in the glaze.

5. A rejection mechanism is at work in this precipitation which is not chemical in nature.

6. The glaze requires a free-flowing liquidity which reduces the syrup-like gel to a more watery state, that is, which reduces viscosity. Maximal liquidity is achieved by eliminating alumina in the glaze and by using sodium, lithium, or potassium in a zinc glaze frit. As active fluxes, they lower the melting point of the glaze. We may say the liquidity gives the zinc or iron particles freedom to swim.

7. At maximum heat the metallic particles swim, or agminate. The term "agminate" means to gather in clusters.

8. The agmination starts with a "push" that is rejection, and it may end up with the "pull" to a metal center from which crystals grow after they have clustered. Dissolution takes place at maximal heat, as molecular relationships are destroyed.

9. The cooling process produces crystals. Zinc combines with silica, which is crystallizing to form zinc ortho-silicate.

10. Either a slow or rapid cool will produce good crystals. The kiln temperature may be dropped as follows:
    a. Cone 11 dropped to 2075° or more.
    b. Cone 10 dropped to 2020° or more.

c. Cone 9 dropped to 1900-1950° or more.
The lowered temperatures are usually held for three or more hours.

11. Jim Kempes, an Abiquiu, New Mexico, potter on the staff at Ghost Ranch, has ventured a daring move: "After the hold, increase the temperature a little so that the growth of the crystals will have its final last fling in an increase of liquidity."[43]

Glaze crystals grow best on smooth, non-ribbed pots. As a zinc glaze cools, a polarity often forms from the center, with lines striving to express a third dimension on a flat surface as if trying to rise off the surface of the pot. Many of the crystals are round, as though drawn to a central, nucleus-like magnet.

Crystal shapes defy the imagination. Heat is a factor, time is a factor, so are gravity, electricity, and magnetic pull. The final result expresses the new systematic organizing forces which take place when old relations are destroyed. As if by magic, in the struggle of both zinc and silica to crystallize, a new structure emerges, organized into patterns and beautiful to behold.

Glaze application is of critical importance. The glaze must be thick, as much as one-sixteenth inch. Application may be by usual methods of brushing, spraying, dipping, and pouring. A thicker application at the top of the piece and a thinner one at the bottom is good. Spraying and dripping upside down is best in order to achieve this.

It is inevitable that thick glazes, as they cool in the kiln, run toward the bottom of the piece. A plan for keeping the glaze off the kiln shelf is imperative. The following techniques have been helpful.

One method is to place under the pot a circular piece of insulating firebrick the same diameter as the base of the pot. The top rim of this firebrick piece is brushed with kiln wash, a fifty-fifty creamy mix of kaolin and silica. Another choice is to place a pile of 60-mesh Ottowa silica sand under the pot. The sand is poured on the shelf in a pile high in the center. The pot, with its base coated twice with kiln wash, is placed on the sand so that its weight flattens the sand to form a pile whose top matches the diameter of the bottom of the pot.

The best method is to throw on the wheel a shape to contain the spilled glaze. It is shaped like a flattened bowl with a candlestick type of center on which the pot is placed. The thrown piece must have the same diameter as the base of the pot. After the bisque fire, the pot is glued to the base by a mixture of equal parts of white glue and alumina hydrate. Kiln wash may be used on the contiguous areas which are glued. The glue is placed on the areas to be sealed to one another. Excess glue is removed. After the piece stands a while, the pot may be lifted, and the base will adhere as the pot is glazed. After the pot is glaze-fired, the base is chipped off with a chisel, although in many cases the chisel is not needed. Superflow glaze on the pot bottom requires a grinding wheel.

The Aventurines

Historically, the aventurine glaze, also known as the Goldstone, is not an old glaze. In 1300 in Murano, Italy, artists made brown glass flecked with brass filing known as aventurine glass. The term aventurine is from an Italian word meaning chance or accident, and it refers to the accidental discovery of a means of incorporating flat spangles in glass. The term has come to be applied to crystals or spangles in glaze on clay that look like a gold flake. Referring to this glaze, C.F. Binns once said—with Rookwood Tiger Eye Goldstone in mind—that it ranked with the fine art productions that made the old Chinese so famous.[44]

The Indian Hills Glaze

When living at Indian Hills, Colorado, in 1954, I saw iron crystalline glazes fired at about 1940°F. The glaze I later developed in a small electric kiln matured at about 100 degrees hotter (Cone 02).

I began with certain known factors, which fortunately held true. I used procedures outlined in criteria for discovery that mentioned the required overload of iron, and a basic flux that would express the rejection principle in the glaze, some one chemical that would either reject or give them the least opposition for swimming into a coalescence. For this element I selected borax, since it worked in the iron crystalline I had seen. And since silica is the basis of all glass, I felt it would facilitate the rejection principle. Thus I confined the ingredients to three, with a wild guess as to the amounts of each.

I tried these three ingredients—iron, borax, and silica—without success. I was reading Browning's "Abt Vogeler," who was extemporizing on the musical instrument he had invented. I changed the word "note" in the original poem to read "gram":

Consider it well, each gram in our scale, in itself is naught;
It is everywhere in the world—loud, soft, and all is said
Give it to me to use! I mix it with two in my thought
And, there! Ye have seen and heard: consider and
bow the head.[45]

Then I added a fourth line:

That out of three sounds he frame, not a fourth sound but a star.

I decided to add the fourth glaze ingredient as a "star." This star was to be the so-called Eye of the Tiger Goldstone. I fired twenty formulas, and one of them had a lone tiger eye. It was from nepheline syenite, the Canadian spar that is a dominant soda-potash-type spar.

The glaze was far from finished. I decided to increase each ingredient on a systematic basis (see "Four-component System" in Chapter 18, Examples of Tests). From this process, I secured crystallizations and took the best one. Using this recipe, I tried fourteen more derivations in the same fashion. This improved the glaze. The new improvement was used in a new set of fourteen mixes, giving a brilliant galaxy of gold spangles. (An iron crystal forms as either a spangle or a flat flake. A spangle reflects gold in its light. It is like a galaxy of stars.)

The Indian Hills Glaze Recipe

I usually add to the frit 2% of barium carbonate and 4% of kaolin for the following recipe. This induces redness and stability.

Cone 02 Aventurine

Borax Glass	35.5
Silica	34
Red Iron Oxide	17
Nepheline Syenite	13.5

Zinc Crystalline Glazes

I had tried prior to 1956 to get a Cone 2 (2125°F) zinc crystal. In fact, I had tried at least a hundred mixes. One of the problems was in dealing with five ingredients, because they add up to many possible combinations.

For the fluxing chemicals I had tried sodium and boron to reduce viscosity and increase liquefaction and glaze flow. This would precipitate the zinc, which could not dissolve in the silicate to agminate, that is, to form clusters with their own identity. This was not a rejection principle; it was an enabling principle. The given chemical boron or soda would enable the zinc to swim well in the molten silica.

A Guest of Importance

The tourist season would soon be over, on September 15th, but when another visitor came into the studio I felt some resentment. Why take time out for another interruption of a busy morning? However, an appeasing influence prevailed, and I told the visitor to take over as though he owned the place and really nose around. Then I forgot him completely until he came back with purchases. The gentleman said, "I see you're working on glaze crystals." "Yes," I said. "The iron does well, but I can't make zinc crystals large enough. I could do more if I could decide whether to use sodium or boron." His unforgettable reply was, "I am Clarence Jeglum, in charge of research for the Philadelphia Quartz Company. I will send you the Kraner research papers showing zinc crystals using sodium silicate. You might throw out the boron."

This started me on a series of experiments using sodium silicate in powdered form and a continuing correspondence with Dr. Jeglum.

Cone 2 Zinc Crystal

Powdered #20 Sodium Silicate	32	Titanium Dioxide	6
		Nepheline Syenite	8
Silica	18	Bone Ash	3
Zinc Oxide	22	Copper Carbonate	3
Lithium Carbonate	8		

Glazes Tried With Commercial Frits - Cone 10
Held at 2020°F or less for three hours to form crystals.

Frit 283 (Pemco)	42	Frit 757 (Pemco)	48.2
Zinc	22	Zinc	19.8
Silica	20	Silica	32
Titanium Dioxide	5		
Lithium Carbonate	5		

Frit 3819 (Ferro)	52	Frit 3110 (Ferro)	52
Zinc	22	Zinc	24
Silica	26	Silica	24
Titanium Dioxide	6		

Frit 283	68
Zinc	24
Silica	8

Glaze Frit From Author's Recipe - Cone 11
Held at 2050°F or less for three hours to form crystals.

Lithium Carbonate	3.9
Potassium Carbonate	16.9
Zinc Oxide	26.35
Silica	52.75
Nickel Oxide	2.0

Snair Glaze (from **Ceramic Monthly,** *December 1975) - Cone 9*

Frit 3110	48.40
Zinc Oxide	24.35 (calcined)
Kaolin	1.52 (calcined)
Silica	17.95
Titanium Dioxide	7.78

High Temperature Iron Crystal - Cone 10

Frit 283 (Pemco)	50
Silica	14
Red Iron Oxide	24
Lithium Carbonate	12

This iron glaze is strikingly effective. Applied in thick and thin areas, it produced one of our first high-temperature Goldstones with amazing tiger eyes.

Note On Fritting: It must be repeated that fritting is necessary. It is a means of melting a glaze twice—first in a crucible then on the pot. I developed an excellent method of fritting, which is described in the Addenda. I always frit everything but the color, including zinc and silica in its entirety. Commercial frits are preferred by most potters.

31

SIMPLE GLAZES USING ASH

Piñon Tree Ash

A student brought to one of my workshops some piñon ash that formed a glaze by itself. This was the starting point for building a beautiful ash glaze. We started with three ingredients in equal amounts—feldspar, piñon ash, and kaolin, as suggested by Bernard Leach. We got an alligator skin effect. To reduce the refractivity of the glaze, we tried 35% ash, 20% kaolin, and 45% feldspar. This gave us a glaze with the required gloss. (If the glaze runs, reverse the process by adding kaolin at the expense of feldspar.)

To improve texture, color, and stability of the glaze, we added dolomite, talc, and colemanite, believing the magnesia present would do the trick. The colemanite as an active flux would balance the more refractory fluxes. We felt zinc would improve color and opacity. The recipe follows, expressed in grams:

Piñon Ash	35	China	35	Talc	7.5
Potash Spar	23.2	Dolomite	3.5	Colemanite	6.5
Whiting	3	Zinc	1.5	Red Iron	1.3

This produced a yellow glaze. Where extra thick under reduction conditions, it went into a deep, muted green. Where very thin on a brown body, the color of the body determined the tone of the glaze color. Obviously, the best results from this glaze were obtained by varying thickness of application using hand brush or an air brush.

Another suggested starting point for a stoneware ash glaze is 40 parts feldspar, 10 parts whiting, 10 parts kaolin, and 40 parts ash. If the result requires gloss, one may decrease ash or kaolin. If it runs too much, one may decrease fluxes or add kaolin.

My piñon ash was derived from the fireplace. All starting kindling was of the same wood, and people who might toss in paper, cigarettes, or orange peel were warned by a sign not to do so. The ash was first run dry through a normal door screen. It was then mixed with water and stirred thoroughly. This mixture was allowed to stand for 24 hours, after which the excess water was poured or decanted off to remove caustic and soluble materials.

Water was then added and the ash was screened through a 60-mesh screen. The water was drained off after settling, and then the ash was dried in the sun or on tin sheets over a radiant heat. When thoroughly dry it could be weighed as a glaze component.

32

NATURAL ORE GLAZES

I once visited a potter in Central City, Colorado, who experimented with the many natural ores of the area. He used natural silicates like the petuntse stone used by the Chinese. The impurities included commercially valuable metals such as gold, silver, zinc, and lead. The glazes formed a galaxy of brilliance with unusual crystallizations. Many of the effects existed only on samples rather than on pots. Some could not be duplicated. His wife was an excellent wheel artist, and he had beautiful glazes on some of her work. The glory was in the experience rather than in the production of finished examples.

I started working with some of the Colorado ores that are commercially produced on the market today. The joy in this was in getting to meet the small producer who operated alone in the mountains or in conjunction with a very small company. This sentimental approach was the drive behind these research efforts. Within the thrill of the experience, one sees unfolded the heart of what these basic materials really are. They create their own methodology in a kind of on-the-spot intuitive response as to what one might do with them. One man supplied me with all of the beryl and amblygonite needed.

I found an elongated rock crystallized into a hexagon in an abandoned feldspar mine. This was beryl. Was it curiosity that impelled me to use beryl, or was it something I had read to the effect that it stabilizes green colors from copper? Travelling from Tiny Town, Colorado, on the road west, I found an ore which, mixed with frit, gave beautiful spangles of gold. This was a micaceous hematite. The micaceous shape of this mineral in an iron compound reflected gold. The fun was in trying it, in looking for an answer. The material is the method. The method is the material.

Many potters may think they don't have natural ore readily available. Once some boatmen, lost in the mouth of the Amazon River, dying of thirst, did not know they were in the fresh waters of the river's mouth. A passing plane signaled, "Put down your bucket where you are." I have heard tell of a marine biologist finishing his kiln and his adobe studio who began with a glaze made from the adobe in his house.

33

SINGLE-FIRE CERAMICS

Most artist potters have to fire twice. There is a bisque fire under 2000°F and then a gloss fire, usually over 2300°F. To fire only once represents an enormous saving of fuel and labor. It will suffice here to recount some personal experiences of potters.

I used the single-fire process for seven or eight years. There were no failures as such from this process, though the incidence of breakage was naturally higher. For this process the amount of the clay in the recipe must be limited. The process does not appear to tolerate more than about forty percent of a plastic clay. Using less plastic clays, like fireclay and kaolin, the clay content might approach fifty percent or slightly more. Obviously, the process works if the quantity of clay is reduced, but this decreased the green strength of the piece. Other factors include the fact that the work glazed must be of a fairly thin, uniform wall thickness. A few artist potters are making quantities of pottery by the single-fire process.

The piece glazed on the inside must be allowed to dry for several hours before it is glazed on the outside. It cannot be handled without risk until it is dry. Pouring glaze into a pot if the glazing is done rapidly has proved workable. It is, however, preferable to apply the glaze with a gun. An overthick application may crack the piece. I've glazed one-fire work by dipping. Much is yet to be learned of this process. Slip-cast pottery is more easily glazed while green than is wheel-thrown pottery, because the clay content and wall thickness can be minimal.

I know of current experimentation with a clay recipe as follows:

25%	Plastic Clay	12%	Potash Feldspar
20%	Edgar Plastic Kaolin	14%	Talc
10%	Sand or Grog	14%	Silica

More research is needed. The challenge of single firing is tremendous. The risks are great, but the problems, though considerable, can be solved. Single firing promises an enormous saving of labor as well as of fuel. It can be done, it has been done, and it needs to continue to be done. Pioneering and taking risks are part of success in this venture.

34

MEDIUM-FIRE CERAMICS

Clay Bodies

I was required in the early development of my art to work at medium-range temperatures, only up to about Cone 2 or less (2130°F or less). After many years of working with stoneware and porcelain bodies with glazes maturing at Cone 10 (2375°F), I was forced to a reassessment of values.

The medium-range clay body and special glazes are worthy of more emphasis. With greater work in this area, new merit will be found in medium fire for clay and glazes. We face a continuing need for energy conservation, which requires us to consider the value of firing pots at lower than the generally high temperature range of Cone 10. One potter reports that he was able to cut natural gas fuel costs by 74 percent when moving from Cone 9 to Cone 3.

In considering a lower temperature, the primary decision for the potter is whether or not lower temperatures mean lower standards. There are adjustments and changes of standards which come with the low-temperature fire. Medium fire brings some losses of values and also some attendant gains.

Cone 2 clay bodies may be semivitreous, although there is shorter vitrification range. They are dense, strong bodies, though not quite as strong as the high-temperature bodies forming mullite crystals.

The following clay bodies at Cone 2 are near to vitreous, strong, white-burning, and safe. They are sufficiently workable. They could contain less ball clay and more fireclay if aged. They have been used considerably, but they are too high in clay content for a single-fire operation.

A P Green Fireclay	15	Lincoln Fireclay	17
Kentucky #4 Ball Clay	45	A P Green Fireclay	17
Talc	10	Kentucky #4 Ball Clay	36
Feldspar	10	Talc	10
60 Mesh Sand	10	Feldspar	10
		60 Mesh Sand	10

Glazes

Medium-Fire Glazes

Many friends throw up their hands at the idea that great ceramic glazes can be made at, for example, Cone 2. In this, we do not have the weight of tradition and practice. Most potters, not seeing evidence of great Cone 2 glazes, are skeptical. A truth well known among a few potters is that excellent glazes with a variety of chemicals are useable. In no case are lead, soluble fluxes, or frits necessary, as is the case with low-temperature glazes.

Not so well known is the fact that superb crystalline glazes in both iron and zinc can be made at this temperature. We just haven't seen much evidence because they require fritting. The author, a generation ago, fritted zinc and iron crystal glazes in this range that equal anything he has been able to make at Cone 10.

On the question of zinc crystals for Cone 2, the role of the usual soda frits used for high temperature crystals has not been fully explored, but the fritted crystals I used prove that their use is feasible.

Use of Zinc in Non-Crystalline Glazes

During the nineteenth century, lead poisoning among potters at Bristol, England, became a major concern. Zinc oxide glazes in the Cone 4-6 range were developed. They were resistant to abrasion and chemical attack. Good greens and blues were obtained, but the iron colors were lifeless.

High-zinc glazes produce fine opaque mattes. While there are attendant losses of some desirable characteristics, a beautiful mottled effect is possible from using zinc. For purposes here, we may use zinc in the Cone 03-3 range by supplementing small amounts of other fluxes. Also, zinc may be used effectively in lower percentages with several fluxes in workable combinations.

The recipes included here are glazes in which colemanite, lithium, barium, calcium, and zinc are used. These are the effective fluxes. Each of these may be used in sufficiently large quantities to give special quality to the glaze. While they may be the dominant factor in fluxing the glaze, other fluxes in smaller amounts are used in various combinations. The use of lithium reduces crazing (cracks) in the glaze. More effective than potash spar is nepheline syenite and volcanic ash. The latter is more responsive at lower temperatures than the nepheline mineral, which, in turn, is more responsive than potash feldspar in this range. Potash feldspar is useable. The following are production glazes developed and used in the Ghost Ranch Experimental Seminars. These soft, waxy mattes are recommended, although some further adjustments may be needed if they run.

Cone 2 Barium Matte Pale Green

Lithium Carbonate	3	Silica	16
Zinc Oxide	5	Custer Feldspar	36
Whiting	10	Barium Carbonate	30
Colors: Rutile - 4		Tin Oxide - 4 Copper Carbonate - 1	

Cone 2 Colemanite Matte Blue Lavender

Silica	28	Rutile	4
China Clay	8	Tin Oxide	4
Colemanite	40	Copper Carbonate	1
Whiting	18		

Gloss Texture - Cone 2-3

Gerstley Borate	32	Silica	20
Zinc Oxide	7	Custer Feldspar	35
Whiting	5	Bentonite	1
		Rutile	4

Volcanic Ash Glazes (Cone 1-3)

Volcanic Ash	Colemanite	Kaolin	Whiting
75	25		
65	22	8	5

A host of recipes are derived from the use of Kansas, New Mexico, and Mt. Saint Helen's volcanic ash, which work equally well with various fluxes, requiring somewhat less of them than nepheline syenite.

Slip Glazes

Albany Slip	80
Gerstley Borate	20

For Greenware

Barium Carbonate	4
Gerstley Borate	12
Opax	12
Talc	24
Lithium Carbonate	10
Calcined Kaolin	20
Kaolin	10
Tin Oxide	8

Burnt Orange - Cone 1-3

This is a starting point for Albany slip glazes and slips with a burnt orange effect. Experimentation is suggested to increase matte or gloss effects.

Albany	30	50	Albany	43.5	40
Dolomite	12	10	Gerstley Borate	6.2	24
Gerstley Borate	20	25	Lithium	43.5	6
Nepheline Syenite	28		Talc	3.7	
Ball Clay	10	10	Zinc	0.12	
Barium Carbonate		5	Ball Clay	3.1	
			Barium Carbonate		4
			Bone Ash		8
			Dolomite		18

Zinc Glazes

Nepheline Syenite	Lithium Carbonate	Zinc Oxide	Whiting	Silica	Titanium Oxide	Barium Carbon.	Ball Clay	Cone
16.5	12	20	4.5	38.3	7.5			1 clear matte
22	10		5	38	7		17	2

Lithium Glazes

Lithium Carbonate	Zinc Oxide	Whiting	Silica	China Clay	Cone	Type
26.9			53.5	13.6	02	Gloss
22.1	7	11.3	30	28.1	02	Clear Gloss

ADDENDA

ADDENDA

I. THE RED RECIPES THAT WORK

A small group of American potters have succeeded in producing high-temperature copper reds. Doubtless they have been besieged by requests for their recipes. Each one has a favorite. In comparing these recipes we find wide differences.

Reds are a basic reaction to oxygen reduction rather than to chemicals. Many recipes will work satisfactorily. However, evaluation of recipes to arrive at simple standards resulting from potters' experiences is worth doing, though not much has been done. Research has been woefully inadequate for several reasons. Various recipes relying on reduction have to be placed in close proximity at the same level and position in the kiln. Added testing in another firing does not represent the same kiln atmosphere. Engineers and potters alike have not generally met these requirements—or have not been in a position to attempt adequate research.

Many of the reported results suggesting the value of a given ingredient have to be discounted. A result interpreted as chemically favorable is usually a function of kiln atmosphere. Nevertheless, some potters, as mentioned, have favorite recipes. These recipes, it must be borne in mind, worked in a particular type of kiln with a given reduction cycle. Ideally, one should, when borrowing a recipe, have a kiln capable of a similar reduction cycle. By way of encouragement, once the recipe and cycle function well, the results in a stable kiln with a capable fireman can be depended upon in a production program of red glazes.

Here is an evaluation of ingredients:

1. Calcium Carbonate. It is the most widely used of any of the fluxes.

2. Boric Oxide. Also widely used.

3. Barium Carbonate. It has a darkening effect on glazes, particularly if used over ten percent.

————— 159

4. Zinc Oxide. It may brighten color.

5. Magnesia. Talc and dolomite, though not indispensable, are often used in small amounts.

6. Tin Oxide. Without tin, the reds are worthless. Tin reduces copper and stabilizes the glaze.

7. Iron Oxide. Iron in very small amounts also assists in the reduction of copper. It is worth trying on an experimental basis. There is considerable precedent for iron in Chinese glazes.

8. Lithium Carbonate. A valuable ingredient, though not essential or widely used.

9. China Clay. It will give glaze stability. If used, it must be in limited amounts. Alumina seems a deterrent in reds.

10. Feldspar. Various potash feldspars—soda feldspar and nepheline syenite—are basic. One may substitute one for another with freedom, providing the lower fusion point of soda spar and nepheline syenite is kept in mind.

Following is a table of limits drawn from a larger number of successful recipes:

	_P B W_
Potash and Soda Feldspars	30-50
Calcium Carbonate	10-20
Silica (depending upon spar amount)	10-30
Talc	2-6
Borax Glass or Colemanite	6-12
Barium Carbonate	4-8
Zinc Oxide	2-3
Kaolin	2-4
Tin Oxide	1-2
Copper Carbonate	0.5-1
Iron Oxide	0.4-0.9
Lithium Carbonate	1-3

Two high-whiting glazes rely primarily upon only one or two fluxes in addition to the feldspar family. The first is the glaze Walter Donald Kring, ceramic artist and minister, has preferred for thirty years:[46]

Feldspar	43.9
Flint	18.1
Whiting	20.1
Florida Kaolin	3.7
Kentucky Ball Clay	11.3
Tin Oxide	0.8
Copper Carbonate	0.6

This glaze, high in alumina and whiting, can be taken to Cone 12. The high-whiting lithium glaze of George Wettlaufer, ceramic engineer and artist potter, follows:[47]

C-6 Feldspar	30
Spodumene (ceramic)	20
Whiting	20
Silica (super-sil)	25
E.P.K. Clay	5
Copper Carbonate	1.5
Tin Oxide (0.5-2)	0.5

These glazes are recommended for their simplicity and the alkalinity factor:

	Willard Spence	*Harding Black*
Nepheline Syenite	40	
Custer Feldspar	10	
Silica	25	75 Soda Spar
Whiting	10	12
E.P.K. Clay	2	
Colemanite	12	12
Copper Carbonate	1	1
Tin Oxide	2	1

Harding Black of San Antonio, Texas, has a recipe for a complex glaze.[48] By a strange coincidence it is very similar, except for the addition of zinc, to one of the author's glazes, which was arrived at independently.

	Black	*Spence*		*Black*	*Spence*
Potash Feldspar	21	23	Whiting	8.5	10
Nepheline Syenite	21	29	China Clay	4	2
Colemanite	9	10	Silica	22	17
Talc	2	3	Copper Carb	1	1
Barium Carb	5	5	Tin Oxide	1	2
Zinc Oxide	3	0	Lithium Carb		1

It might be interesting to put 0.5 percent of iron in this glaze. The following glaze used in Japan is a high-barium glaze. By eliminating the tin and increasing the copper carbonate to three percent, one may build blue tonality.

Nepheline Syenite	60	Silica	7
Barium Carbonate	27	Copper Carbonate	1
Lithium Carbonate	2	Tin Oxide	2
China Clay	6		

The above, reduced fairly strongly, may give a red-violet matte glaze.

Glazes with kaolin, colemanite, and barium dominance follow.
The following glaze, high in colemanite, may be used at Cone 8 or 9.

Kingman Feldspar	21
Silica	22
Nepheline Syenite	30
Colemanite	16
Barium Carbonate	9
Whiting	2
Copper Carbonate	1
Tin Oxide	1.5
Red Iron Oxide	0.5

Cover Glazes

The use of cover glazes is promising. Harding Black insists that the old Chinese techniques included cover glazes and that the Sang-de-Boeuf is essentially an "underglaze" phenomenon. He uses his soda red glaze without tin and copper for the cover glaze. Almost any red glaze can be used as cover by omitting the tin and copper.

Glazes without color, including those high in alumina and whiting, should be tried. A high kaolin glaze impedes running. Following is a high-alumina and whiting glaze:

Silica	33
Whiting	20
Potash Feldspar	27
Kaolin	20

The cover functions as a protection from oxidation and noxious gases. The effect often appears as a strong silicate reaction.

Unquestionably the Chinese used celadons for cover glazes. This offers the possibility of iron as a reducer (as well as tin as a reducer in the underglaze red). Iron coloration augments the red color, permitting a thinner application of the red underglaze. It should be noted that iron was basic in small amounts in the Chinese glazes.

A celadon cover glaze with lithia, alumina, and whiting content is as follows:

Lithium Carbonate	8
Whiting	16
Kaolin	21
Silica	55
Red Iron Oxide	2

Used by itself, the above is a beautiful, soft green celadon. The cover glaze is applied very thinly, or it can be used with less iron where there is thicker application. Another application is to use two regular Sang-de-Boeuf recipes, both with copper and tin. A glaze dominant in a particular chemical should be used over a glaze dominant in another one. For example, take recipes high in whiting, barium, lithium, or colemanite and apply one over the other. Results from this are often quite exceptional.

Donald Pilcher, who makes excellent reds, suggests putting a runny glaze over a refractory glaze. One may experiment with glazes maturing above or below a general Cone 10 goal. For example, the aforementioned Kring glaze could go to Cone 12. The glazes of Laura Anderson contain over fifteen percent kaolin. Glazes that mature at Cone 8 or 9 could be tried as cover. Some of these are high in colemanite. One possibility is feldspar 25, silica 25, nepheline syenite 25, colemanite 17.5, barium carbonate 10, whiting 2.5, copper carbonate 1, and tin 1 percent.[49]

It must be remembered that the five-layer theory shows a blue color immediately under the red. Blue functions naturally under the red, and interesting results may be obtained by putting a high-barium copper glaze under the Sang-de-Boeuf. Similar to a blue used by Carlton Ball is the following:[50]

Nepheline syenite	47
Barium Carbonate	37
Ball Clay	7
Rutile	9
Copper Carbonate	1

The Japanese red glaze in this chapter may serve in this blue capacity by omitting the tin oxide called for in the recipe and using three percent of copper carbonate.

II. GLAZE CALCULATIONS

Ceramic engineers usually reduce a glaze to a molecular equation. The ceramist doing this needs a briefing on the chemical background. In most cases, it may be preferable not to use these glaze calculations.

Most people today realize that our universe is composed of atoms. There are now known to be at least 92 basic chemical elements. The finest unit of each element is the atom, each with a specific weight. Particles of each pure element are alike in both weight and size. They are indivisible and indestructible. Each has a proton with a positive electric charge for a nucleus around which circulate in orbital motion small negatively charged electrons. These basic atomic units of matter enter into chemical union with other elements, forming compounds. Such unions are called molecules. These combinations follow simple ratios, such as one to one, one to two, or two to three. Water, for example, is formed from two atoms of hydrogen and one atom of oxygen (H_2O). The atomic weight of hydrogen has been selected as 1.0080. Two atoms weighing 2, combined with one atom of oxygen weighing 16, give a total weight of 16 plus 2, or 18, for one molecule of water.

The molecule is the smallest unit of a given substance or compound. When one element unites with another, the combination always takes place between a definite number of each kind of atom. When water forms, the percent of oxygen and hydrogen is always the same. There is something significant in the fact that in the compound forming water the ratio of 2 to 16 or 1 to 8 is always the same. Water by weight will always have eight parts of oxygen to one of hydrogen. All the chemical elements combine in the ratio of their combining weights or in simple whole multiples of these. This fact has established for physics the law of multiple proportion.

Sir Thomas Dalton established the atomic theory on the fact that, "[i]n a series of compounds that are made up of the same elements, a simple ratio exists between the weights of any one element that combine with a fixed weight of another element."[51]

Valence is the property of an atom that enables it to combine with a certain number of atoms of another element. Sodium chloride, NaCl, represents one atom of chlorine with one of sodium, and a valence of +1 and -1. Aluminum oxide, with a valence principle of 2 and 3, is expressed chemically as Al_2O_3.

Molecular Structures

All the matter that makes up the earth is composed of the smallest pieces of the approximately one hundred chemical elements that we call atoms. Each has distinctive characteristics. These elements do not occur in nature in a pure form but in compounds, which are groups of atoms held together by an electrical attraction or bond. The atom is much too small to be weighed, but it was possible to determine the relative weight of one type of atom to that of another. Oxygen, symbolized by the letter "O," was given an arbitrary atomic weight of 16. Other atoms were given a weight corresponding to their proportionate weight relative to oxygen.

Silica, mentioned frequently in the chapters on clay and glazes, is a major ceramic compound and is found in every clay and glaze. The molecular formula for silica (more correctly silicon dioxide) is SiO_2. This indicates that the compound consists of one atom of silicon and two atoms of oxygen. From the atomic weight table we find that the weight of silicon is 28. The two oxygen atoms weigh 32, thus yielding 60 as the molecular weight of the compound silicon dioxide (silica).

Silica may be added to a clay body or glaze in the silicon dioxide form but is most commonly found as a part of a more complex compound such as kaolin or feldspar.

In industry and in large studios, glazes are most often developed using empirical calculations. The formulas resulting are chemically accurate and allow for a uniform repetition of the glaze, which is often needed when recipes are altered. An empirical formula shows the number of molecules of each oxide used to give a glaze. Obviously, all empirical data must be changed to a batch recipe. The process is simple. The requirements of each oxide in the empirical formula are multiplied by the number of their molecular (or equivalent) weight.

The molecular weight of an oxide or chemical compound is the total sum of the atomic weights of its constituent elements. Some elements appear more than once in their own empirical formula. In such cases, the equivalent weight of the compound is used in calculations. The chemicals are classified by ratio of oxygen, the arbitrarily chosen letter "R," resulting in three columns as follows:

Monoxides		Tri-Oxides		Di-Oxides	
RO or R_2O		R_2O_3		RO_2	
Lead Oxide	PbO	Alumina	Al_2O_3	Silica	SiO_2
Zinc Oxide	ZnO	Boric Oxide	R_2O_3	Rutile	TiO_2
Potash	K_2O			Tin Oxide	SnO_2
Soda	Na_2O			Zirconium	
Whiting	CaO			Oxide	ZrO_2
Barium Oxide	BaO				
Magnesia	MgO				
Strontia	SrO				

The monoxides in any empirical formula should form a unit total of 1.0 as follows:

K_2O	0.3	or	K_2O	0.3
CaO	0.3		CaO	0.7
ZnO	0.2			1.0
Na_2O	0.2			
	1.0			

The following form is convenient for glaze calculations:

	K_2O	CaO	Al_2O_3	SiO2
	0.3	0.7	0.5	4.0
0.3 Potash Feldspar	0.3		0.3	1.8
	xx		0.2	2.2
0.7 Whiting		0.7		
		xx		
0.1 Raw Clay			0.1	0.2
			0.1	2.0
0.1 Calc. Clay			0.1	0.2
			xx	1. 8
1.8 Fling				1.8
				xx

"The empirical formula calls for .3 equivalents of K_2O, so .3 equivalent of potash feldspar is required. When .3 equivalent of potash feldspar is added, there are also added .3 equivalents of Al_2O_3 and .3 x 6 or 1.8 equivalents of SiO_2. The .1 equivalent of raw clay supplies .1 equivalent of alumina and .2 equivalent of silica. The other glaze ingredients are considered in a similar way."[52]

The following are rules for a shortcut operation in conversions to empirical formulae. These represent batch weights already derived from multiplication by equivalent weights.

Rule 1 - When taking out 56 parts of potash feldspar, add 26 parts ball clay and 24 parts flint. At the same time add one of the following materials in the amounts named: 26 parts white lead, 8 parts zinc oxide, or 10 parts whiting.

When adding 56 parts of potash feldspar, take out 26 parts ball clay and 24 parts flint. At the same time take out one of the following materials in the amounts named: 26 parts white lead, 8 parts zinc oxide, or 10 parts whiting.

It should be obvious that multiples or fractions of the number call for proportionate changes in the other values listed.

Rule 2 - Leaving feldspar alone: when taking out 56 parts white lead, add 8 parts zinc oxide or 10 parts whiting.

When adding 26 parts white lead, take out 8 parts zinc oxide or 10 parts whiting.

Rule 3 - Leaving feldspar alone: when taking out 8 parts zinc oxide add 26 parts white lead or 10 parts whiting.

When adding 8 parts zinc oxide, take out 26 parts white lead or 10 parts whiting.

Rule 4 - Leaving feldspar alone: when taking out 10 parts whiting, add 26 parts white lead or 8 parts zinc oxide.

When adding 10 parts whiting, add 26 parts white lead or 8 parts zinc oxide.

Rule 5 - When adding 26 parts ball clay, take out 12 parts flint.

Rule 6 - Flint may be taken out or increased without paying attention to any other material. Even if a glaze has no flint, the rule still applies.

Rule 7 - To make a matte glaze from a bright or glossy glaze, take out flint by Rule 6, allowing, however, for the flint figure in Rule 5, because ball clay is to be added by Rule 5. Add whiting by Rule 4 at the expense of white lead.

Rule 8 - If calcined Florida kaolin is used instead of ball clay, replace each 26 parts of ball clay by 22 parts of calcined Florida kaolin.[53]

III. THE FRIT KILN

Glazes are classified according to whether they are raw or fritted. A fritted glaze is one which is melted twice. The first time it is pre-fired in a container to a melt and then re-ground to a fine powder. It is melted a second time on the pot in the kiln. A frit, then, is a pre-melt and dual melt.

In general, the potter looks askance, feeling that fritting is only for industrial operations, having all sorts of far-fetched ideas about the chemical equations that go into a glaze frit. We propose herein to give a very down-to-earth answer, a basic simplification of what goes into a frit, so that a potter who is not chemistry oriented need not be perplexed by the frit's challenge. The approaches discussed herein will endeavor to answer the following two questions: How to frit— how much trouble is it really? Why frit—do we really need to go to the trouble?

The answers supplied are encouraging. First, the potter can build the right kind of equipment at low cost and complete the operation with minimal work and time. We've not had the positive answers because we have been stymied by lack of knowledge of simple, workable equipment. Equipment mentioned has been antiquated, difficult, cumbersome, and time-consuming. Let's begin with the second question—Why do it?

Why Frit a Glaze?

Let's take an imaginative look at what happens when a glaze is placed in a container and melted. Suppose we put a raw glaze into the proposed frit kiln which will mature on a pot at about 2385°F (Cone 10). This material heated in the container will begin to shrink, harden, and coalesce 500 degrees or more before the Cone 10 heat. The ingredients with the lowest melting point, the fluxes, will act on the other ingredients. The fluxes, in order of their meltability, will melt and attack the higher fusible materials, silica, alumina, and others. This is basically a process of dissociation that, as it progresses, will turn the glaze into a stiff, syrupy liquid, still 300°F or more below the Cone 10. This liquid, though stiff, will form a glass and, like molten lava, will move more slowly when pulled by gravity.

The lava-like substance, doused suddenly in cold water while red hot, will sizzle and form minute cracks. Then the cracked material may be ground to a fine powder in a ball mill in about 8-12 hours, depending upon the glaze and the temperature at which it was fritted. What are the changed characteristics of the frit? Toxic substances in the frit combined with the silica lose practically all of their toxicity. This applies to all such materials as lead, barium, cadmium, and copper carbonate. Caustic ash materials, pearl ash, soda ash, and others are much more easily handled as frits.

Lead is the most dangerous ingredient, so lead frits which are applied to containers for food and drink should still be tested for lead solubility before being used. Many glaze ingredients dissolve in water. This is particularly true of boric acid, raw borax, sodium carbonate, and potassium carbonate. Note further that many other materials are slightly soluble in warm water or in acid. Copper carbonate dissociates in hot water; cobalt carbonates dissolve in acids. With added heat the cobalt decomposes readily. The glazes containing the aforementioned solubles are insoluble as a frit.

The tendency for a glaze to crawl is reduced in frits. The frit, being through the cooling phase as a pre-melt, will have a smoother, more perfect surface. Fritted glazes are also more homogeneous. A raw glaze settles to the bottom more easily than a frit. In the latter, all the ingredients are the same weight. We correct settling by use of one percent of bentonite. In a frit we lower the melting point of the glaze. Also, barium and some other fluxes are more active when fritted.

Soluble materials in a non-frit glaze applied to a pot with underglaze decoration on it tend to lessen the brilliant color and delineation of the underglaze. A number of colors in glazes are more brilliant in the frits. Fritting brings homogeneity, color, general stability, and freedom from defects not found in a raw glaze. On the other side of the coin we need to recall the brilliant alkaline glazes of Persian antiquity, and many others, where mastery of the use of soluble materials was in evidence. Certainly many caustic and poisonous glazes are handled safely through the use of gloves, ventilated booths, and other precautions. These facts in mind, many potters use solubles and toxic materials with aplomb.

Frits Available

There are several manufacturers of frits. Some manufacturers freely disclose the contents, usually in the form of a molecular equation. This data is available in a number of ceramic books. One of the most complete is THE POTTER'S COMPLETE BOOK OF CLAY AND GLAZES, by James Chappell.

In the pros and cons of fritting there is one final observation. If one can get results not possible by any other means, then fritting is a viable option. If one requires a recipe not available, then it is wise to make one's own.

The potter's questions are: Where am I and where do I wish to go? Basically, each potter determines a unique program and inquires whether fritting should be a part of it. The situation determines the need and includes such possibilities as: (1) the need to fire at low temperature range when lead and the alkalies need to be fritted; (2) the need for a very low-temperature frit to be mixed with wood ash glazes for lower than 1900°F (raku glazes may be fritted); (3) the need for stability and color in general appearance of the glaze; (4) the need for specialized programs such as crystal glazes; and (5) the need for a frit adaptable to medium- or high-temperature needs.

The Frit Content Spectrum

What does one put into a frit furnace and what can one put in? There are broad extremes forming a spectrum. On one end is a well-balanced glaze with alumina, silica, fluxes (monoxides, di-oxides, and tri-oxides) in correct balance. On the other end of the spectrum we may have frits which are basically fluxes—no alumina—and small amounts of silica. The potter may read Rhodes, Parmellee, and other authors who discuss criteria for well-balanced glazes using molecular equations.

In general potters revel in their freedom, and freedom they have. One may frit raw borax by itself or with silica. Lead with silica is possible. All sorts of things are possible. Rules are made to be broken, but keep in mind that broken rules exact penalties and create problems. Certainly reason should be thrown to the winds. Normally, glaze requires silica and alumina for strength and balance. Frits for reduction reds or crystals dispense with the need for alumina. There are some very limited problems for a frit low in silica, although silica is easily added to a frit. Many potters like things out of balance. There is wide freedom to add to a glaze. Adding clay will give alumina and also serve as a suspending medium.

There is another question relative to a well-balanced glaze. When is a frit a complete glaze? Working at this point in the spectrum, one may build a complete glaze which theoretically requires nothing to be added. Yet even here we do not quite have a complete glaze. Glaze color is added, and something to hold the glaze in suspension; also, gums to add strength and adherence.

How To Frit A Glaze

In general, the fritting methodologies have been cumbersome to the extent of discouraging many potters' attempts to frit. This holds true at the academic as well as the industrial level. One method suggested in textbooks is use of a pan-like sagger coated with silica, with no suggestion of the type of furnace. The frit is fired and the silica is scraped off. Then it is crushed in an iron mortar and ground in a ball mill.

There are suggestions for use of a crucible with a hole in the bottom fitted with a plug. Draining the frit by removing the plug is possible, but replacing it and refilling the crucible while hot is a difficult operation. Other methods include lifting the crucible from the kiln and draining. Firing equipment shows two burners hitting the crucible on opposite sides or one burner entering at the base, angled to put gases around the kiln in a circle as they travel upward.

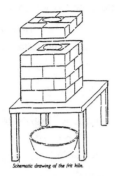
Schematic drawing of the frit kiln.

The method suggested herein offers marked savings in efficiency and time. A crucible is used that is heated in an electric kiln with a chamber nine inches square. The crucible has a hole in the bottom from which the frit drains while it remains in the furnace. It then drains through a larger hole in the bottom of the kiln. It drops into a tub of cold water, which shatters it or cracks it so that it can go into the ball mill without pre-crushing. The only preparation for the ball mill grind is to dry the frit thoroughly. The crucible is refilled through a hole in the top of the kiln slightly smaller than the diameter of the top of the crucible. One can determine the need to refill by looking in the top kiln hole. When the crucible is one-half or one-third full, add more frit.

Before putting the initial frit into the crucible, one moistens enough of it to roll it in the palm of the hand and makes a compact ball. The ball is placed in the inside of the crucible over the hole in the bottom. The frit does not fall out of the bottom until the ball is melted, which permits a gradual exit of the frit into the tub.

The only labor involved is checking the switches of the electric kiln, replenishing the crucible every half hour or so, and cooling the water every two or three hours when it is warm. With practice, one could frit while doing other things in the studio. The operation can be a joyful sojourn. In my Colorado studio, I would prepare enough of the two frits I used to last a year.

The frit is really a spit furnace. The frit ejected, shaped like icicles, is red hot until it hits the bottom of the water tub. Usually snow or ice is shovelled into the tub two or three times. The routine can be varied by card playing, pipe smoking, etc. When finished with the fritting, one should keep strong heat on the crucible to thoroughly empty the residue from the side walls. There is no other way to clean the crucible. If a different type of glaze is fritted, a different crucible is used. This requires cooling down the kiln to make the replacement.

The Crucible

The dimensions suggested here for the crucible are nine inches high with a top outside diameter of six and one-half inches and a three and one-half inch diameter at the bottom. The bottom hole is one inch in diameter, which could be enlarged (only if needed) to one and one-eighth inch. To make a crucible is risky, as one broken in operation could ruin the furnace. Commercially made crucibles are safe and last for years unless dropped. As a precaution, it should be fired and cooled gradually. The crucible rests on a collar three and one-half or four inches in diameter. Two collars this wide are useable, with the crucible resting on one two inches high on the kiln floor level. Collar and crucible can rest on a second collar going through the kiln floor. The collar through the floor may rest on a refractory support on the table. It may be supporting the weight of the crucible and frit. Conceivably, one collar could be used. Collars may seal to the crucible from frit flow, but they are still useable. An alternative to a collar going through the kiln bottom is a homemade fire clay shelf with a hole in it on the kiln floor. Since the height of the kiln interior is twelve inches, the kiln shelf and collar should total about two inches, leaving one inch between the top of the crucible and kiln lid.

In order for frit drippings not to touch the kiln bottom, there should be minimum inside diameter of three inches for collars or holes in the floor. The lid hole is covered with an insulating fire brick. For refilling the furnace in operation, one needs only a quart coffee can bent into a funnel shape and a pair of asbestos gloves.

Furnace Proper

The furnace proper is converted to an experimental kiln by plugging lid and bottom holes with Kaowool. Used in the kiln are K-23 insulating firebricks. Brick for sidewall, laid flat, is sealed with high-fire bonding mortar. Five layers of brick give the inside height of twelve inches. Grooves in the brick are designed to hold Kanthal wire and made prior to kiln construction. In laying the brick, use staggered bond.

It is best to enclose the kiln with a band of plumber's tape around each layer, tied with a turn-buckle. Many may prefer to purchase an electric kiln of slightly different size, converting it to a frit furnace. Crucible sizes can vary some. The hole in the floor and lid may be made before or after construction. The lid can be tied together with plumber's tape. The floor should also be tied together.

To get a good fit of sidewall to floor, the floor can be made first. The sidewall is made resting on the floor, but it should not be sealed to the floor. By similar token, the lid may be made by resting the brick on the sidewall.

The Table

The table top is about two and one-half feet or less above the tub. It has crosspieces of wood on which are placed hard firebrick to support the furnace and crucible.

How to Grind a Glaze

The glaze frit is useless until ground to a fine powder in a ball mill. Ball mills utilize a revolving horizontal cylinder in which the frit is ground. The frit is ground by impact between the ball-like grinding medium which is caused by the rotation of the jar. Jars of a size suitable for the potter's use should be a foot or slightly more in outside diameter. Given a very small operation, a smaller jar is preferable. For a larger quantity of frit, a larger jar is needed.

Some potters may have enough time, skilled help, and desire to save money to make their own ball mill. The suggestions following are for the potters so desiring. The grinding jar may be thrown on the wheel using a vitreous stoneware or a porcelain. This requires a skilled thrower. The outside diameter should be approximately twelve inches, or more depending on skill and needs. The length should be about one-and-one-half times the diameter. It should be about five-eights inch thick. Porcelain jars on the market usually run one hundred dollars or more. The jar has a neck shaped to be able to hold a wood cover inside the neck. The outside neck contour should face in, so that a steel bracket can be secured over the top. This bracket has a screw in it that tightens on the lid. Between the wood lid and the jar is a piece of round rubber, which may be cut from an inner tube.

Ball mills have been called pebble mills because they utilize for grinding media pebbles ground smooth by river action. They are roundish or oval, varying in shape, and must have a smooth surface. A flint rock is best for its hardness. One may purchase these, look for them in a riverbed, or even sort them from piles of rock in a commercial gravel company yard.

I used a pebble combining the merits of both the aforementioned shapes. To create one, roll in the hand a round ball of stoneware clay and fire it to vitreous hardness. Using hand pressure it is rolled hard and dense. It is then placed on a smooth surface. One comes down on it with a rectangular, smooth piece of wood about the dimension of the human hand. The wood held parallel to what the clay ball is on is pressed until the ball is about one-half inch thick, or about one-third the diameter of the piece. The result is a thick disk. This shape has more impact surface than the commercial cylinder, and it is very easy to make. The surface must be smooth.

The pebble size for a jar of about twelve by eighteen inches would be one and one-half inches in diameter and one-half inch thick. One can find natural shapes in gravel piles or even in a driveway.

Ball mills are called roller mills because the jar is rotated on two rollers, one activated by an electric motor. The best rollers are of hard rubber with a steel shaft approximately one-half inch in diameter. Rollers require a search. They may be purchased new from a commercial house or used from a print shop. Small mills have been taken from washing machine wringers found in antique shops or second-hand stores. The rubber roller should be about six inches longer than the jar. The roller diameter for a twelve-inch diameter jar should be a minimum of two and one-half inches, preferably more.

Each end of the shaft is secured in a wood frame with a sleeve bearing between the shaft and the wood. One shaft must be long enough at one end to permit a pulley for a V-belt. If it is too short, it may be extended by a sleeve or by welding on a longer piece. Bearings may be purchased from roller bearing shops.

The correct speed of rotation of the jar is essential. This will be such that the pebbles fall from the top of the jar to the bottom, making major impact. If the speed is too slow, the pebbles slide and do not get to the jar top. If the speed is too fast, they circulate all the way around the jar without falling. When the jar RPM is correct, one hears the noise of impact. The normal jar revolutions per minute for jars of twelve-inch diameter is about 70. The motor for a twelve-inch diameter should be at least one-third horse power. It should be capacitor-type, and 1725 RPM is useable. The motor pulley diameter most practical is two inches, with V-belt attached to the pulley on the roller, which may be four or five times the diameter. The roller will turn the same speed as the roller pulley. The motor can be on the same wood frame as the roller and jar.

The Ball Mill Operation

The grinding media should not take more than half the area of the jar interior. The amount of frit should be such that when the mill stops there is no excess frit above the surface of the pebbles. Grinding time varies with the hardness of the frit and the fineness desired. One can usually get a fine mesh in a cycle of six to twelve hours. One potter gave up fritting because of the time involved in emptying the mill and cleaning it. He was grinding wet frit. Converting to a dry frit, it is possible to empty the mill in a half-hour or less, with no cleaning required and frit and pebbles separated.

To screen frit from pebbles, use a coarse screen with square holes one-fourth inch or more in diameter. A household colander six inches in diameter will work. Just shake it, and in a few seconds a colander of frit and pebbles will disgorge all the frit. By using dry frit, one can load and unload the mill in an hour. It needs no checking other than a check for spillage, heating motor, or motion of the jar toward one end of the frame. To avoid the latter, the mill should be absolutely level. The main hazard is the noise. It is best to work in a separate room.

IV. ADVENTURE WITH KILNS

KILNS IN GENERAL

Heat Energy

The experience of kiln building is an adventure that may end in triumph or tragedy. The love of building as a venture and as a means of lowering cost is the reason many potters build their own kilns. Many homemade kilns produce severe results, such as uneven heating (hot bottoms, hot corners, cool corners) or the inability of the kiln to reach sufficient temperature. Many potters spend a year getting their homemade kilns to work. Among the requirements for success one must consider:

1. *Insulation-* The heat must not be lost through the walls but stored to build increased temperature.

2. *Combustion-* There must be fire-power, BTU energy sufficient for creating and storing heat for a given kiln size.

3. *Structure-* Walls and ceiling must be adequate for structural support.

4. *Design and Shape-* These must permit maximum loading capacity and permit heat circulation. Kiln failures are most often due to inadequate fire-power or insulation.

There are three methods of transferring heat: radiation, conduction, and convection.

Radiant Heat- This refers to heat transfer through space, irrespective of matter. Energy is radiant energy and not heat until it travels through material. The radiant energy of the sun reaches us in eight minutes (due to the speed of light). We don't understand the nature of these electromagnetic waves. The former kilns that used long cylindrical tubes to convey heat to pots may have been chosen because of the large radiant surface for multidirectional radiation.

Convection- This is heat transfer in liquid hot gases due to change in density. Heat gases expand, decreasing density, and travel upward, being drawn into dense areas. This may push cold air down to replace the warm air that has moved up.

Conduction- This is heat flow through matter. If a hot body and a cold one were in a vacuum, the hot one would radiate energy to the cold one. The amount of heat radiated is in direct proportion to the difference in temperature. It is also proportional to the area through which it can flow. There are several factors involved in heat transfer by conduction:

1. Emission is the heat coming off the hotter body.

2. Absorption of heat is receptivity of the cold body.

3. Equilibrium is the state where heat flow results in similar temperatures for the emitting and absorbing bodies. Time is also a basic factor in this. Time produces an isothermal condition.

4. Insulation is the opposite of conductivity. This is resistance to absorption of the material. Heat is absorbed slowly and is conducted through the body slowly. In terms of insulation, the potter deals with materials that could be classified as excellent, good, fair, or poor. Heat travels through fibrous materials that may be troweled on to a kiln or a Kaowool blanket. While traveling through two and one-half inches of insulating firebrick, it may travel through seven to nine inches of hard firebrick.

5. Heat loss is costly.

6. Fusion is the means of rating kiln materials in terms of temperature limit. Above their limit, kiln materials may fuse, disintegrate, become misshapen and render the kiln nonusable. For example, the hot surface of a brick may be insulated with Kaowool, which is rated industrially with high temperature limits, e.g. 2400°C - 2600°F.

On the cold surface of a brick, which is several hundred degrees cooler, one may find a trowel-like insulation material workable. There are excellent materials available that would be damaged above the general 1900°F range. Insulating firebrick is referred to by a K-factor corresponding to the temperature limit of the brick in terms of 100°F. A K-23 insulating firebrick is useable up to or slightly beyond 2300°F.

Circulation of Heat

The ingress, usually at the bottom, is the opening or openings where oxygen and products of combustion enter. As the heat travels up, maximal heat is adjacent to or immediately above the combustion area. At the top in updraft, the hot air escapes upward. These convectional currents build velocity, and as the height of the kiln is increased, the possibility of cooler portions of the kiln at the top is increased.

The downdraft kiln pulls these hot gases down to the floor, where they exit to the trough leading to the stack. The stack is a natural draft because at its top the atmosphere pressure is less than at the bottom. Air rushes up through the stack's natural pull and it pulls from the kiln gases that are reversed from upward flow to downward flow. This system utilizes heat more economically and distributes heat more evenly. Circulation must be such that heat is distributed evenly through the pottery. An isothermal condition (equilibrium) has to be established within tolerable limits through the area of loaded pottery.

Combustion is the interaction of carbons with oxygen, forming a flame. The area for combustion must be large enough to permit full realization of the hydrocarbons and oxygen as they ignite and interact through the flame.

Heat Convergence

This is the principle by which the area of the cross section of the kiln is reduced to compensate for the reduction of temperature. The bottle-kiln, for example, grows smaller as it extends upward. The ancient Ching-ti-chen kiln grows smaller as it extends horizontally.

KILN TYPES

Downdraft Slow-Time Cycles

The Ching-te-chen Kiln

This kiln requires a stack. The hot gases are pulled somewhat downward through an area of convergence of heat resulting from reduced space to be heated.

The Oriental Chamber Kiln

The chamber kiln has a natural uphill topography. Each unit is a complete downdraft unit. The initial unit can be turned off when temperature is attained. Each unit has evenness of heat due to downdraft retention of heat, and a long time cycle that permits an isothermal condition. When combustion is started in the second chamber, adjacent to the first, it has already attained sufficient temperature to tolerate heavy feeding of wood.

The Round Downdraft Kiln

This kiln has a long time cycle and downdraft. It is shaped like a beehive.

Primitive Kilns

The Dung-Type Fire

1. The pots are built into a circle, touching one another.

2. Cow chips are laid horizontally over the pots, closely adjacent to one another, forming an igloo shape.

3. The chips reflect heat inward and oxygen enters between chips. Heat is circulating through the pots rapidly.

Speed of heat and extent of opening is controllable by placing chips over one another.

The Metal Rack Fire

1. One layer of pots may be placed over a rack with a fire built underneath.

2. Pueblo Indians may build two racks, using tin cans as shelf support posts.

3. Dung may be laid against the rack for a side wall.

The Metal Pan Container

1. This method has evolved from firings supervised by Jim Kempes at Ghost Ranch, Abiquiu, New Mexico.

2. The container is a large barrel end with a rack under it supported by firebricks.

3. This system requires a pit under it into which the sticks are fed from openings at opposite ends.

4. Pots are first preheated by varied means, after which a small, slow fire, maintained for some time, is built under the container. This usually eliminates breakage from moisture in the pots.

5. The pit permits stick-fire on all sides of the pan, and with a lid on the pan, sticks are piled on top.

6. The fire progresses in this order: (a) underneath, (b) on sides, and (c) on top.

7. There is a gradual buildup to a large, intense fire from bottom, sides, and top. Any dry stick is useable, which eliminates the need for cedar or dung.

8. After the stick fire dies, the lid is removed and pots removed by tongs. Pots are left in for firing black and the lid is replaced. The pan is covered with damp straw or sawdust, which smolders for two to three hours.

Raku Kilns

The Ghost Ranch Shuttle Kiln

The chief value of this kiln is the dynamic group experience made possible. When the rack is pulled out, those removing ware must be dressed for protection from heat radiated. Two on each side, with varied-type tongs, depending on the shape of pots to be removed, are pot removers. Four, standing behind removers, are required on each side of the rack to place the pots under buckets of straw or excelsior, etc. Some pots are dunked in water by others after buckets are removed. In this kiln, progress of heat is observed through peepholes or through the removable openings at the top of the door. Prior to firing raku, pots are preheated on top of the kiln. From this point they can be quickly placed on the emptied rack for each new firing. When the cart is pushed all the way into the kiln, its back frame closes the kiln tight. This kiln was built from drawings made by the author.

The Soldner Raku Kiln

This kiln is lifted off the top of the pots. It may be constructed large enough for several pots or small enough for only a few.

The Garbage Can Raku Kiln

This kiln is lined with fibre insulation (Kaowool or other high-temperature material). The practical values of this kiln are:
1. Saving money due to insulation.
2. Saving time (it can be heated and cooled quickly).
3. Permitting focus on the special needs of only one or two pots.

V. HEALTH HAZARDS

Health hazards are very real. We do not hear much about potters who have developed problems, but there are more than the general public realizes.

Silicosis

This is a hardening of the lungs from breathing materials which are high in silica. Clays are hydrated aluminum, over half silica by weight. Silicosis takes at least ten years to develop. It can cause shortness of breath, dry cough, emphysema, and high susceptibility to lung infections such as tuberculosis.

Materials other than clay have silica content: feldspar, talc, vermiculite, perlite, volcanic ash, Cornwall stone, nepheline syenite, grog, sand, and several others. Materials used in glazes contain silica also. China clay dust can cause not only silicosis but mechanical clogging of the lungs.

Hazards and Precautions

The commonest hazards are from mixing clay and glazes, but many other phases of handling spread dust in the air: sanding of clay can create a problem, and small pieces of clay on the floor become pulverized and are an inhalation hazard. Reconditioning of clay is a hazard. Following are some precautions:

1. Mix clay outdoors if possible.

2. If not possible to mix outdoors, secure manual ventilation.

3. When pouring a clay or a glaze material that arouses dust, hold your breath and move elsewhere until the dust settles. Take similar precautions when adding materials that create dust to water.

4. Wear an approved dust respirator whenever there is a hazard involved.

5. Clean up floor and tables with wet sponge or mops. Industrial vacuum cleaners with wet pickups are helpful. Hosing the floor is good.

6. Do not continue to wear dusty clothes, particularly shirts. Closely woven synthetic material does not entrap as much dust as cotton clothes.

7. Clean up discarded clay each day. Do not allow it to dry.

Asthma-Type Allergies and Skin Problems

Wet clay is handled when one wedges, sours, ages, shapes, and dries clay. The most serious problem, not common but very real, is an asthma-type allergy to molds that grow in clay. Clay aged for months and longstanding clay slips have theşe problems. These molds can also cause skin problems, particularly if there is a pre-existing dermatitis. Precautions include adding a preservative to clay. If you want the mold to grow, avoid inhaling clay containing mold.

Wear gloves whenever possible when handling clay. Using a barrier cream on your hands is helpful. Normal use of clay does not pose this hazard so much as does opening a fresh container of moist clay and breathing it.

Lead

Lead, red lead, white lead, galena, and litharge are all poisonous. Avoid raw leads if possible by using lead mono-silicate, bi-silicate, or sesqui-silicate. Lead should not be used in high-temperature glazes for other reasons: it is volatile and leaves scars on pots. Leadless glazes can be used for low-fire conditions. Medium-fire glazes, 2000-2200°F, do not require lead. Zinc was the first common substitute developed, in glazes called Bristol glazes. Toxic glazes came from the high incidence of lead poisoning in England in the late nineteenth century (see Chapter 34, Medium-Fire Ceramics, for lead-free chemicals). There are laws against lead glazes. For tableware such a glaze is a hazard, particularly if the glazed piece contacts high-acid foods.

186 The Potter's Odyssey
186 — The Potter's Odyssey

Precautions

Use a mask when working with lead. Wear gloves. Wash hands thoroughly. Avoid getting glaze on abraded or sore skin. Work where there is ventilation or, best of all, out-of-doors. If you spray a raw lead glaze, you may have difficult problems. Have a good blower system, or work outdoors with a current of wind blowing away from you. In all cases, wear a mask and gloves.

Skin Hazards

Sieving ashes or ash glazes can dissolve alkaline substances from alkaline water. Skin contact with this causes irritation. Other skin irritants include potassium dichromate, soda ash, potassium carbonate, and fluorspar. Use the precaution of gloves with these materials. The material can cause skin problems whether wet or dry. Barrier creams can't usually be used, since they cause a glaze to crawl during the firing process.

Ceramic Colorants

1. Uranium oxide, chrome yellow, zinc chromate, and other chromium compounds can cause lung cancer if inhaled.

2. Cadmium, lead, antimony, and vanadium compounds are toxic.

3. Antimony oxide, chromium compounds, vanadium, and nickel compounds are moderately toxic by skin ingestion.

4. Commonly known for toxicity are barium carbonate and copper carbonate. Most of the colorants in glaze are not hazards if common sense is used. Avoid breathing dust when mixing and weighing and applying glazes. The use of a mask may be necessary. Most glazes are applied with greater ease by dipping, pouring, and brushing. This eliminates the need for a spray gun, which should only be used in a booth with a blower mechanism and a fan.

Kiln Hazards

Fuel-fired kilns are heated by wood, coke, and charcoal. All of these fuels produce carbon monoxide and other combustion gases. To remove these gases, fuel-fired kilns are usually vented at the top. During the early stages of firing—between 500 and 800°C (932 and 1472°F)—the organic matter in clay is oxidized to carbon monoxide and other combustion gases, and carbonates, chlorides, and fluorides break down to release carbon dioxide, chlorine, and fluorine gases. Sulfur, found in many clays and other materials, breaks down between 1000 and 1100°C (1832 and 2012°F) to produce dense clouds of sulfur oxides. Nitrates and nitrogen-containing organic matter in clays also break down to release nitrogen oxides. Glaze ingredients which can release these gases include galena, Cornish stone, crude feldspars, low-grade fireclays, fluorspar, gypsum, lepidolite, and cryolite. At stoneware firing temperature and above—starting around 1150°C (2100°F)—certain metals, including lead, antimony, cadmium, selenium, and the precious metals, are vaporized. At these temperatures, nitrogen oxides and ozone can be produced from oxygen and nitrogen in the air.

Even salt glazing, which involves placing the bisque ware in the kiln and throwing wet salt into the heated kiln, reacts to form large amounts of hydrogen chloride gas.

Hazards

1. Chlorine, fluorine, sulfur dioxide, nitrogen dioxide, and ozone—all of which can be produced during kiln firings—are all highly toxic by inhalation. Acute exposures to these gases are unlikely, except in the case of sulfur dioxide. There have been instances of dense clouds of choking white gases coming off during bisque firings with high-sulfur clays. Inhalation of large amounts of these gases could cause severe acute or chronic lung problems.

2. Regular inhalation of these gases at low levels could cause chronic bronchitis and emphysema, since they are all lung irritants. Fluorine can also cause bone and tooth problems.

3. Carbon monoxide produced by gas-fired kilns and from combustion of organic matter is highly toxic by inhalation, causing oxygen starvation. One symptom of carbon monoxide poisoning is a strong frontal headache which is not relieved by aspirin.

4. Hot kilns produce large amounts of heat, and direct contact with the kiln can cause severe burns. Hot kilns also produce infrared radiation which can be an eye hazard—possibly causing cataracts—when you look inside the kiln to see if the pyrometric cones have bent.[54]

Precautions

Wear approved welding goggles or hand-held welding shields to protect your eyes when looking inside the kiln. A shade number of between 1.7 and 3.0 should be adequate, but check for spots in front of your eyes after looking away to be sure. Didymium lenses are industrially approved.

NOTES

CHAPTER 1

1. Davis, Harry. "Art, Commerce and Craftsmanship. An Historical Review." *Ceramics Monthly*, December 1981.

CHAPTER 2

2. Spence, Willard M. "The Emergence of the Artist Potter in the Twentieth Century." Unpublished paper. Department of Art, University of Denver, 1955.

3. Honey, W. B. *The Art of the Potter*. Faber and Faber, London, 1944, p. 48.

4. Read, Herbert. *Art and Industry*.

5. Honey, op. cit.

6. Leach, Bernard. *A Potter's Book*. Transatlantic Arts, Inc., 1953, Chapter I.

7. Browning, Robert. "Rabbi Ben Ezra." *Robert Browning's Selected Poems*. Ed. Charlotte Porter & Helen A. Clarke. Thomasy Crowell, New York, 1906.

8. Leach, Bernard. *A Potter's Portfolio*. Putnam, 1951.

9. Sempill, Cecilia. *English Pottery and Porcelain*. Collings, London, 1947, p.47.

10. Leach, Bernard. *A Potter's Book*. Transatlantic Arts, 1953, p. 6.

11. Billington, Dora. "The Younger English Potters." *Studio*, 78-83.

12. Billington, Dora. "The New Look in British Pottery." *Studio*, January 1955, p. 18.

13. Robineau, Adelaide Alsop. "Founder." *Design*, Nov. 1937, p. 37.

14. Ibid, p. 7.

15. Hughes, Robert. "Review Exhibition Whitney Museum." *Time*, January 18, 1982.

CHAPTER 3

16. Leach, Bernard. op. cit.

17. Wildenhain, Marguerite. *Craft Horizons*, May 1953, p. 43.

18. Pillin, Palia. "Pottery." *Arts and Architecture*, November 1948, p. 35.

19. Robineau, Adelaide Alsop. "Potter of Topanga Canyon." *Craft Horizons*,

20. Wallace, George. "Old Man Teague." *Modern Maturity,* AARP, Long Beach, April-May 1983.

CHAPTER 8

21. Ramie. "Picasso as Potter." *Craft Horizons,* Summer 1950.

CHAPTER 16

22. Saunder, Dr. Herbert H.

CHAPTER 19

23. Collie, J.N. "Notes on the Sang-de-Boeuf and the Copper-Red Chinese Glazes." *Transactions of the Ceramic Society,* Vol. 17, 1917-18, pp. 379-384.

24. Ibid.

25. Hobso, Robert L. *Chinese Pottery and Porcelain.* London, The Stourton Press, 1934.

CHAPTER 22

26. Mellor, J.W. "The Chemistry of the Chinese Copper-Red Glazes." *Transactions of the British Ceramic Society,* Vol. 35, 1936, p. 373.

27. Ibid.

CHAPTER 23

28. Ibid., pp. 364-378.

CHAPTER 24

29. Hetherington, A.L. *Chinese Ceramic Glazes.* Cambridge University Press, Cambridge, 1937, p. 42.

30. Ibid., p. 40.

31. Mellor, op. cit.

32. Ibid., p. 367.

CHAPTER 25

33. Wettlaufer, George. "Copper Reds for Potters." *Studio Potter,* Vol. 8, No.1, January 1980, p. 24.

34. Ball, Carlton. "Copper Red Glazes." *Studio Potter,* Vol. 8, No. 1, January 1980, p. 28.

35. Grebanier, Joseph. *Chinese Stoneware Glazes.* New York, Watson/Guptill, 1975, Chapter 7.

36. Black, Harding. Personal correspondence with author.

37. Kempes, James. Interview, Abiquiu, New Mexico.

CHAPTER 29

38. Grebanier, op. cit.

39. Hetherington, A.L., op. cit.

40. Simon, Sandra. "I Like Porcelain Because Blood Shows Up Better On It." *Studio Potter,* Vol. 6, No. 2, 1978, p. 32.

41. Coleman, Tom. "Working With Porcelain." *Studio Potter,* Vol. 6, No. 2, 1978, p. 4.

CHAPTER 30

42. Stull, Ray. *Transactions of the American Ceramic Society,* 1903, Vol. 5, 6, p.186.

43. Kempes, James. Interview.

44. Binns, C. F.

45. Browning, Robert. "Abt Vogeler."

ADDENDUM I

46. Kring, Walter Donald. "Copper Red Glazes." *Studio Potter,* Vol. 8, No. 1, January 1980.
47. Wettlaufer, George, op. cit.
48. Black, Harding. Personal correspondence.
49. Coleman, Tom, op. cit.
50. Ball, Carlton, op. cit.

ADDENDUM II

51. McNamara, Edward P., op. cit.
52. Parmelee, Cullen W. *Ceramic Glazes.* Industrial Publications, Chicago, 1951, pp. 53-54.
53. Cox, Paul E. "The Use of Iowa Clays in Small Scale Production of Ceramic Art." *Iowa State College Bulletin,* Vol. 24, No. 44, 1937, Ames, Iowa, pp. 33-34.

ADDENDUM V

54. McCann, Michael. *Artist Beware.* New York, Watson/ Guptill, 1945, Chapter 10 on Ceramics, Glassblowing and Enameling.